Monica Furlong

Monica Furlong has written biographies of Thomas
Merton, Alan Watts and Thérèse of Lisieux and a book
about contemplative prayer. She has published five
novels, three of them for children.

MONICA FURLONG

Flight of The Kingfisher

A Journey Among the Kukatja Aborigines

Flamingo
An Imprint of HarperCollinsPublishers

Flamingo
An Imprint of HarperCollins*Publishers*
77–85 Fulham Palace Road,
Hammersmith, London W6 8JB

Published by Flamingo 1997
9 8 7 6 5 4 3 2

First published in Great Britain by
HarperCollins*Publishers* 1996

ISBN 0 00 638125 1

Set in Linotron Galliard
at The Spartan Press Ltd,
Lymington, Hants

Printed and bound in Great Britain by
Caledonian International Book Manufacturing Ltd, Glasgow

To Coral and Joseph,
who are still children of the Dreaming

white man got no dreaming,
Him go 'nother way,
Him got road belong himself.

Muta, a man of the Murinbata people

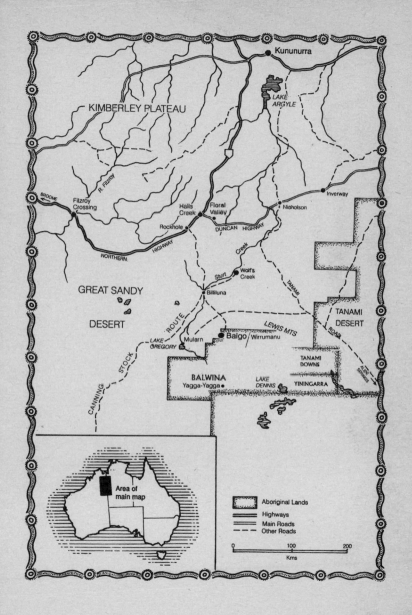

Kununurra

KIMBERLEY PLATEAU

LAKE ARGYLE

R. Fitzroy

BROOME

Filzroy
Crossing

Halls
Creek

Floral
Valley

Inverway

Nicholson

Rockhole

DUNCAN HIGHWAY

NORTHERN.   HIGHWAY

Creek

Sturt

Wolf's
Creek

GREAT SANDY

DESERT

Billiluna

TANAMI

ROUTE

LEWIS MTS

TANAMI
DESERT

ROAD

LAKE
GREGORY

Mularn

Balgo

Wirrumanu

TANAMI
DOWNS

BALWINA

Yagga-Yagga

LAKE
DENNIS

YININGARRA

CANNING   STOCK

Area of
main map

Aboriginal Lands

Highways

Main Roads

Other Roads

0   100   200
        Kms

ACKNOWLEDGEMENTS

My gratitude is due to a number of people who enabled me to write this book:

> To the Chairman of the Wirrumanu Aboriginal Corporation for giving me permission to enter the Balwina Reserve, and to stay at Balgo (Wirrumanu). To the people of Wirrumanu who allowed me to live alongside them in one of the most important experiences of my life.
>
> To Fr Brian McCoy, SJ, and Fr Robin Konig, SJ, to Sr Adele and the Sisters of Mercy, to Cheryl and Anita and Margaret, all of whom were loving and supportive in a way I valued very much.
>
> To a number of books which helped me understand what the traditional life of the desert peoples had been up into the living memory of many at Balgo, in particular *Jilji* by Pat Lowe and the Walmajarri painter Jimmy Pike, which had wonderful details of everyday life. Also to *The Teacher's Handbook* of Luurnpa School, to *Desert People* by M. J. Meggitt, a scholarly account of the neighbouring Warlbiri people in the 1950s, to *The World of the First Australians* by Ronald and Catherine Berndt, *The Dreamtime Book* by C. M. Mountford, *Aborigines of High Degree* by A. P. Elkin, *The Rock and the Sand* by Mary Durack, and *Mysteries of the Dreamtime* and *Letters from a Wild State* by James Cowan, which helped me understand the power of the totem. I found Robert Hughes's book *The Fatal Shore* very helpful in giving the background of the tragic and marvellous white history of Australia, and the way it impinged on Aboriginal life.
>
> Finally, my thanks are due to a number of Australian friends – Frank and Cam Ha Sheehan, Linda Walter, Fay Clampitt, George and Shirley Trippe, who offered me wonderful hospitality, and listened patiently while I tried out my ideas on them. I think they know how much I have come to love their amazing and beautiful country, and what a joy and privilege it has been.

Luurnpa, the kingfisher, is the totemic ancestor of the Kukatja people. The Aboriginal name for Balgo is Wirrumanu. Wirrumanu is the name of the track made by the *luurnpa* in the Dreaming when he led the people from waterhole to waterhole.

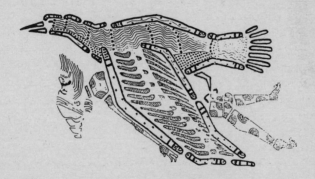

CHAPTER ONE

I travelled to Balgo by way of Bangkok and Perth. At Bangkok I had arranged to stay at a guest house that was a stopping-off place for Presbyterian missionaries, who were speeding through on the way to or from Asia. Missionaries, I discovered, are not like they used to be, or at least like I used to think they were — women in sensible shoes, men in white cassocks — but much more smart, trendy and knowledgeable about the world. Groups of them, many of them very good-looking young Dutch men and women, settled in the living room after dinner and discussed world economic policies and their impact upon poor communities. A nurse, on the way back to Indonesia after a holiday, asked me where I was going.

'Aborigines,' she said, thoughtfully. 'I feel there is something very pathetic about their plight in Australia.'

Aborigines, it seemed, weren't trendy on the missionary circuit. I felt annoyed for them that they should be seen as pathetic, and remembered what Bruce Chatwin's character Arkady had said about them.

'They're very tough, emotionally, and very pragmatic.'[1]

My first visit was to the temple of the exquisite little Emerald Buddha; I thought he was pretty tough emotionally too, not one to be knocked off balance. I loved the huge mirrors in golden frames that confronted

1

me on each side of the Buddha. I asked the guide what they meant, hoping for one of those incomprehensible Buddhist speeches about form being emptiness and emptiness form but, disconcertingly, she told me she wasn't sure. I thought I got the message, however. The plump Western woman with the sore feet and the upset stomach who was seeing herself in the glass was ephemeral. Tomorrow the glass would not show her reflection. And the message, at least for me, was 'Live your life now, this minute. Relish *these* blisters, *this* diarrhoea, this heat, these crowds, that roof in brilliantly coloured tiles, this beggar, that family cooking and washing up in the street, because you are a tourist in this life, and soon the package tour will be over.'

However, despite the philosophy, it was good to leave the traffic jams and pollution of Bangkok behind, and continue onward.

Perth was green, cool and fine. After the loneliness of Bangkok I was meeting old friends, sorting out my digestion, putting together the clothes I would need for the desert. We picked wild figs in a patch of 'bush' that stretched beyond the garden and I ate them sparingly.

My first task in Perth was to send off a fax:

> To John Lee, Chairman of Aboriginal Council, Balgo
> I am writing to ask permission to enter your territory.

Later, I had to fill in a form asking for permission from the Wirrumanu Aboriginal Corporation to enter the Balwina Reserve, the huge tract of Aboriginal land in Kimberley where Balgo and other Aboriginal camps and outstations were situated. I had arrived there by the time I filled in the form, and I don't think anyone was proposing to throw me or any visitor out, but it was a salutary reminder that this was not white Australia.

I had come thirty thousand miles in search, it seemed to me, of a secret, or maybe the answer to a question, only I wasn't quite sure what the question was. I remembered a visit to an Aboriginal settlement – Kowanyama, in North Queensland – in 1985. It had stayed obstinately in my mind and had finally brought me back to Australia, now, years later, this time to visit the Kukatja people at Balgo Hills in the Great Sandy Desert of Western Australia. Kukatja, I was later to learn, was pronounced 'Googajar'.

2

I rang a nun, Sister Barbara, now living in Melbourne, who knew Balgo well, and asked if she had any advice about provisions.

'They might like some fresh fruit up there. I always longed for it. And be sure you've got shoes with thick soles. The ground's terribly hard.'

I asked a little nervously what she thought the temperature would be. This was the 'cool' period, but I had noticed on the weather forecast that the temperature in the Kimberleys was 37°C. Surely that couldn't be right?

'I'd say about 40°,' she said, and my heart sank. I'm not good at heat. My fear of being miserably, intolerably, hot had become the focus of all my other fears about going to Balgo, the general horror of not coping in an alien world.

To cheer myself up, and wanting to do some homework, I went to look at the Aboriginal art in the Perth Art Gallery. I had not yet got my eye in for the 'X-ray' Arnhem Land paintings done in ochres on bark – paintings often of animals, here of crocodiles and flying foxes with elaborate cross-hatchings – nor for the big ochre paintings of Rover Thomas. And only later, at Balgo, was I to learn about 'acrylic' Aboriginal painting and come to appreciate pictures like Clifford Napaljarri's 'Possum Dreaming'. On this first visit I was struck by what were known as 'pukamani', carved poles erected in Arnhem Land when someone died. To those who knew how to read them the carvings revealed characteristics of the dead person. One of them had a large, hanging penis. Maybe, an artist friend of mine suggested later, to annoy the missionaries.

A group of young schoolchildren were being shown round the Aboriginal exhibition and, inevitably, they noticed the pukamani and found it exquisitely funny.

When I began to study Aboriginal art, the works that spoke most clearly to me were the ones designed with at least one eye on the white folk. One was Lin Onus's 'Marralinga' sculpture, the figures of an Aboriginal mother and child caught together in the deadly blast of the British atomic test in Australia. The other was Sally Morgan's 'Greetings from Rottnest'. Rottnest is an island off the coast of Perth where, in the nineteenth century, hundreds of Aboriginal prisoners died of influenza, pneumonia, and other diseases aggravated by cold. Most of them came from hotter climates and they shivered their way to death in the winter weather with no more than a thin blanket to warm them. Rottnest is now a favourite Perth holiday resort and Sally Morgan's painting shows white holidaymakers disporting themselves while below ground lie the foetal skeletons in their unmarked graves.

On the way back from the art gallery I heard voices shouting below the escalators in the town centre and, looking down, saw a small Aboriginal group surrounded by police. One Aboriginal man was the centre of the scene, arguing furiously. The others stood by silently, listening to every word, at times smiling as though trying to look as if nothing unusual was happening. I drew nearer and listened to the conversation. The police, two male officers and a woman, were arresting the man, and trying to do so, in that crowded place, in a way that was as pleasant as such a thing could be, with smiles and quiet voices. It became obvious that they had been looking for him and now they had found him. Perhaps thinking that the woman officer would alarm him least, they left the talking to her, but the man seemed to feel it an insult and burst out into a flood of swearing about 'fucking women'. The police kept telling him to keep his voice down. Then the male officers took over. It soon became obvious that he was beside himself with terror. They were forced to drag him to their van and every inch of the way he struggled and shouted, saying, 'I'm Jimmie Jupiter, that's who I am. I am Jimmie Jupiter,' as if to impress the incident on our minds, or make sure he did not disappear without trace. As they finally bundled him into the van he threw a beer can into the street.

The next day I went to see an Aboriginal film *Exiles in the Kingdom* in which many elderly Aborigines spoke movingly of being uprooted from their traditional country and being 'settled' at Roebourne on the west coast. Unused to the sea, which she had never seen before, one woman's emotional struggle took the form of a nightmare fantasy she had had of 'the sea spirit' fighting the spirits of her people.

The film told a story beginning to be familiar to me of Aboriginal life being destroyed by the uprooting of peoples, by alcohol and by poverty. Employed as cheap labour to work in the mines or with cattle or, in the case of women, to work in the homes of graziers, the Aborigines found themselves laid off when, after the act of 1967 giving them citizenship, their employers were obliged to pay them a proper wage. Other cheaper labour was imported from outside and many lost their jobs and sank into despair.

The film claimed that what was restoring Aboriginal hope and self-esteem was a renewed respect for Aboriginal tradition and for 'the Law', the code of belief, conduct and knowledge taught by Aboriginal initiation. The 'outstation' movement, which took many Aborigines back from the cities to live on their traditional lands, was linked to this dynamic sense of a future at least partly independent of white good will.

That evening I had dinner in Perth with a psychotherapist I knew and we discussed the film. He told me about the theories of Robert Gardner, an Australian Jungian analyst who had tried to make psychological sense of the brutal clash between white and black culture after the white man arrived. He felt that one culture was a sort of inversion of the other – the white culture with its obsession with time and profit and technology; the black culture in its state of timeless stasis. Gardner's idea was that these two groups needed each other to bring about fruitful change.[2]

I wrestled with this, rather optimistic, view of what, to the outsider, often feels like an intractable problem within Australia. Just as much of the world is trying to rethink its attitude to women, 'the feminine' in its classic form, possibly to save itself from destruction by war and its phallic weapons, so maybe, in Australia, the aggressiveness of a very 'male' society (the first white settlements in Australia were almost entirely male) might unconsciously seek a corrective in peoples who are its opposite. But would Aboriginal Australians, who had lived an apparently contented life for thirty to forty thousand years, gain – 'be fertilized' in Gardner's terms – by contact with the restless whites?

A friend drove me to the airport next morning and we passed the site of the Old Swan Brewery.

'That's the centre of a famous dispute,' he said. 'A rich property

5

developer bought the place and is trying to develop it, but the Aborigines say that it is an important site for them, the resting place of the rainbow snake.'

As he spoke, we saw a woman coming along the road towards the site, carrying the Aboriginal flag of red, black and orange.

'She'll be coming to mount guard there,' my friend said. The protester was a white woman, and it struck me as I was leaving Perth – clean, beautiful Perth – after four days, how, the 'arresting' incident apart, I had not seen a single Aboriginal face.

We flew high over Balgo in the Ansett jet from Perth. 'That's it,' said the pilot. There were buildings, all small, set round an oval, and three groups of buildings outside the oval. To one side were red cliffs – a sort of canyon – and beyond it miles of bare desert. I was looking at a country of rose-red rocks and earth. From the high perspective of the jet the country seemed covered in a network of scars.

Later, the pilot said, 'Hall's Creek – old gold-rush town,' and I saw a tiny place with tin roofs, and a metalled road going away from it.

'The road goes to Fitzroy Crossing,' said the pilot, 'and eventually to Broome.' Hall's Creek, I knew, was the nearest town to Balgo.

'How long by road from Balgo?' I asked.

'Three hours. By dirt track.'

A luminous rectangle began to show a long way away on our right.

'Lake Argyle,' said the pilot. 'Site of the Argyle Diamond Mine. The lake's nine times as big as Sydney Harbour.'

I had talked my way into the cockpit by chatting up the stewardess.

'I'm going to stay in a place called Balgo,' I told her. 'I think we pass over it. I'd like to see it from the air but I've got an aisle seat and I can't see a thing.'

'Balgo,' she said. 'That's a very traditional place. A big Law place.' She was curious about why I wanted to go there. I said I was interested in Aboriginal life, and we began the first of many conversations I was to have with white people in Australia – about land rights, racial problems, black and white coexistence.

'The government shells out enormous sums for Aboriginal development, and the next thing you hear the Aborigines have hired a plane and flown to Darwin for the weekend,' she said. 'Other people have to work hard for their money and they resent it.'

6

The plane came down in Kununurra, a small frontier town set among the mountains of the Kimberley Plateau.

'Be sure to appreciate how green it is,' a Catholic Sister of Mercy had advised me before I set off. 'It's the last bit of green you'll see for some time.'

The heat hit like a blow as I came out of the one-room airport, and got a lift into town. The driver, in shorts and bush shirt, had a face scarred with skin cancer. He dropped me at the Quality Inn – a motel like a million others on the face of the earth – and when I got to my room I thankfully turned on the airconditioning, and helped myself to some fruit juice out of the refrigerator. It was too hot to go out. I decided to postpone eating, to go and have a swim in the pool, and to doze until the heat grew less. I telephoned OrdAir, the small airline which was going to take me out into the desert.

'Yes,' said the man who answered. 'Sister Adele told me about you. Be out at the strip at half past seven.'

Later in the afternoon I walked into town, past the innumerable sprinklers that were the explanation of Kununurra's greenness. I noted the solar heating on the roof of the Hotel Kununurra, the bougain-villea and hibiscus, and the brave planting of palm trees down the middle of the road. There were a number of rather new little streets of houses – Kununurra felt as if it had been put up with a Lego kit just this last year – with pleasing names: Silverbox Avenue, Chestnut Drive, Poinsettia Walk, Nutwood Crescent, Hibiscus Drive and Mistletoe Street. I felt as I often feel in the frontier towns of Australia – the old longing for security and civilization against the threat of wilderness, Bournemouth opposed to desert. But rising behind the town were the vivid red rocks, ominous as sleeping dinosaurs, as if the desert was waiting to turn and devour its own.

There weren't many shops, a supermarket, a thriving chemist, a pub. For the second time since I had arrived in Australia five days before I saw Aborigines, a group of young boys and girls sitting on the grass under a tree, to whom an older boy was saying, 'You shouldn't be smoking.' All the girls were puffing on cigarettes.

In the chemist I bought a powerful pair of sunglasses, recommended by the Australian cancer society, and a blister kit. Then I discovered Walkabout, a 'Bush Walker's Shop' as it described itself. The proprietor noticed me eyeing the Akubra hats, traditional bush hats, as worn by the stockmen, with a felt finish made from rabbit's fur. I knew from a previous stay in the bush that they were wonderfully cool and comfortable, resistant to wind and sun, and that I yearned for one of my own. I couldn't resist trying one on.

'It needs to be biggish so that your sweat moulds it to your head,' said the proprietor. 'They're great hats – you can sit on them, stand on them, and they'll still keep their shape.' She found one that suited me and, willing customer as I was, I forked out $89.

She was curious about where I was going in it. Slightly hesitant after the Ansett stewardess, I explained. This woman had a wise, weatherbeaten face, and it softened when I mentioned Aborigines.

'I've had a lot to do with Aborigines and they're a wonderfully reasonable people, you know. Even when they are offered a lot of aggression, they will still try to calm things. Things are better in Australia than they were. Oh sure, we have our racial problems right out there in the road for the world to see, but it's much easier than it was ten years ago. I thought the Mabo decision [the famous and controversial legal decision that acknowledges Aboriginals were there before the British came and, therefore, have rights to land] was right. How can you pretend Australia was *terra nullius* when the British came? There were thousands of Aborigines living here. We can't pretend we came here and found it empty.'

I asked her how she came to be running a shop in Kununurra, and she told me she had originally trained as a teacher.

'Brought up in Kalgoorlie. I got sick of teaching, and another teacher and I decided we wanted to do something different. My brother said a lot of people were going to live up in the Pilbarra where there was nothing, and that they would need things to buy. So we bought up a lot of stuff and drove up there and became – I didn't know the word for it when we started – bushhawkers. I loved that life – I might go back to it one day. Then we came back here and bought this place. My friend had a baby and left and I bought her out. I've done some silly things in my time, but if I can hold it together now, I'm on to a good thing here. Best site in town and Kununurra is expanding fast.'

I walked back to the hotel as the warm evening was coming on, a big moon rising over the Kimberleys, the cicadas beginning to sing. Tiny striped lizards ran into the undergrowth as I approached, and a plaintive bird called.

I took a shower. The brochure adjured me to dress for dinner in what it called 'Kimberley Formal' – collared shirt and shorts, and no thongs. I wore trousers and a coloured shirt, but discovered when I got to the dining room that I was much less formal than the other women who wore silk dresses and a lot of make-up. Spurning the drizzles of mint-scented vinaigrette and the lettuce chiffonade, I asked for plain, grilled barramundi – one of the best Australian fish – and a simple salad with French dressing, and washed it down with Australian chardonnay. The fish was fresh and delicious.

I breakfasted alone in the dining room and had an interesting chat with the taxi driver who took me out to the airstrip.

'Kununurra is growing fast,' I observed.

'I've seen big changes. Been here twenty-eight years. You could say I was one of the pioneers, and now at last it's taking off – tourist industry and all that sort of thing. I'm glad I knew some of the old people. They were real characters.'

At the little airport there was no sign of the pilot from OrdAir, and apart from a few men who were working on a building project outside and kept coming in to use the drinking fountain, there was no one else in sight. Where were the other people who were going to use the flight?

Eventually, a young man appeared in long white socks and shorts.

'Mrs Furlong?'

'Yes.'

'I'm Don. What's your name?'

'Monica.'

'Well, Monica, I'm just waiting for another plane to come in with some stuff and then we'll go.'

'Right, Don. Where are the other people?'

Don glanced around the room, puzzled.

'No other people. Just us.'

Half an hour later he led me out to a tiny twin-engined plane, a Beechcroft Baron. The back of it was full of mailbags, schoolbooks, shoes, a gun, and a bouquet of flowers. It was, I discovered, the weekly mail plane.

'We'll be stopping off at a number of cattle stations on the way, and at Hall's Creek. Get to Balgo mid-afternoon.'

I climbed up across the wing and sat beside Don in front of a dashboard covered in knobs and switches.

'Don't touch any of the switches, will you?'

I promised not to.

'We'll need to keep your door open while we're taxiing. When I tell you, slam it hard and lock it.'

Don checked everything out loud to himself – touching handles, muttering – it felt a bit like someone saying a rosary. We went down the final runway, and I slammed the door and locked it. (Suppose I hadn't shut it properly? I had a picture of being sucked out.) We were off, flying low enough to see all the desert spread before us.

'See that drawer over there,' Don shouted, nodding into the corner. 'The airsick bag's in there.'

We set off across the Kimberley Plateau, over Lake Argyle and a countryside of red rocks. Don shouted to me to note the big dam recently built on the lake. I did not know it until later but Lake Argyle was the site of a very famous land dispute. This was Kija land, and the Argyle Diamond Mine had been built on a very important Kija site, that of 'the Barramundi Dreaming'. The Kija had had a painful history from the late nineteenth century when pastoralists invaded their traditional lands with cattle, and the Kija, not very surprisingly, took to spearing the cattle and eating them. It was the beginning of a bloody and desperate feud. In 1910, the Department of Native Welfare set up 'feeding depots' to discourage the Kija from cattle killing, but when these were sold could only think (in 1955) of forcibly moving the Kija to Fitzroy Crossing, miles away from their own country. Predictably, they have drifted back. In the headier political climate of the last ten years the Argyle Diamond Mine have compensated the Kija by helping them set up a number of communities and cattle stations owned and run by themselves.

Soon we were coming out of mountainous country and into the Great Sandy Desert, its huge red expanse stretching before us. Sometimes there were outcrops of red rock, one so like a giant lizard that it was like a Dreaming story frozen before one's eyes, sometimes a light covering of green lying across the red sand giving an effect of plush velvet.

'The Wet was very heavy this year,' Don shouted.

Sometimes there was a yellowy expanse in the distance that looked as if it might be water, but turned out to be grassland, the close mat of spinifex that is so common in the western deserts of Australia.

Now we were in Jaru country. Since about 1875 when the pastoralists arrived, the Jaru had lived and worked on the white cattle stations, sometimes disappearing for weeks at a time on 'walkabout' as Aboriginal workers were famous for doing, and using the quieter work period of the Wet to carry out ceremonies that were no business of the whites. In the early 1970s the British owners, Vesteys, sold a whole group of stations, and the Jaru were suddenly and massively unemployed and homeless.

Quite soon, Don brought the plane down on a tiny airstrip on the cattle station of Inverway and a couple of young men dressed in cowboy hats and leather chaps drove out in their truck to meet us and pick up their mail. I climbed out over the wing to give Don room to get out and he had a brief conversation with them. At Nicholson, the next stop, a man drove out with two little children.

'Look, John, here's your school books!'

'It's holidays!' John replied indignantly.

'And Martin's gun. You haven't got the car part? Damn. Can't repair the car till we get the part and now it's another week to wait.'

While Don rearranged the freight I asked about the loneliness of living out in the desert.

'Mostly it's not so bad, but during the Wet it rained so hard that we were completely cut off – no radio, no telephone, no planes, nothing. That was really hard.'

At Floral Valley a woman and a little boy came out to get the mail.

'He and I had a bet at who was arriving,' the woman said. 'He said it was the teacher and he promised to kiss me if he was wrong. He never pays up.'

These domestic runways were painstakingly carved out of the bush. At each side of them were low bushes, small yellow and purple flowers and ant beds rising out of the vivid earth. I slipped behind an oleander bush. I was beginning to feel very thirsty. I knew that in deserts you should never move without carrying water with you, since your life could depend on this simple precaution, but I had foolishly thought we would be in Balgo in an hour or so. I worried about food, too. Having got up early and eaten a light breakfast, I knew I would be starving before mid-afternoon.

Back in the plane, Don offered me a swig at his water bottle and I accepted with gratitude.

'Will there be anywhere we can eat?' I shouted.

'What would you like?' he shouted back.

'A ham sandwich. Some orange juice.'

Don radioed ahead to Hall's Creek.

'They'll be waiting for you.'

He nudged me.

'Look. There's Wolf's Crater.'

There was a vast hole surrounded by desert in which a meteor had buried itself.

At Hall's Creek, there was a much bigger airstrip.

'How are you feeling?' asked the man directing the air traffic. 'The last woman who came in on that plane was real crook, I can tell you.' I said I felt fine, and I found some shade in which to eat my sandwich, while Don waited for another plane to arrive with more mail and freight.

We took off again and were now in the country of the Kukatja, a people undisturbed in their traditional way of life in the Great Sandy Desert until the arrival of ammunition dumps in the Second World War moved them further north to Balgo. We were getting near to Balgo now. So much closer to the ground than I had been on the

Ansett jet, it was possible to see the endless repetition of the sand ridges, clean and red, as if swept. We came down at Billiluna, one of Balgo's 'outstations', and then at Mularn. Beyond Mularn was the huge presence of Lake Gregory in flood, trees rising out of the water, the water itself yellow with silt.

A Sister of Mercy who worked at Mularn introduced herself to me. 'I'm Anne. You'll see me again.'

And, finally, we were over Balgo itself – the oval of sand, the school, the church with its small steeple, the houses and lean-tos and the few remaining humpies. We circled and came down, and as I slid down the wing for the last time I suddenly felt hot and tired and shy, and bothered by the flies.

CHAPTER TWO

I suppose when I arrived in Balgo I was actually in love – with something you might call aboriginality. I had a passion to learn more about a people, or a group of peoples, whose knowledge and way of life went back behind the clamour and squalor, the huge unanswered and unanswerable questions of modern civilization. Innocent of our own Judaic/Christian fumblings as a result of their geographical separation, and then separated again by the white man's conviction of their savagery and inferiority, the Aborigines remain to this day, along with a decreasing number of indigenous peoples, without complicity in the modern world. What they have instead is a knowledge of, for example, the sacredness of the natural world, an overwhelming sense of its meaning. The West no longer has this sense and it seems to me to make us infinitely the poorer, to reveal us not as the know-alls we pretend, but as blinded, confused, maybe lost.

This consideration, not surprisingly, came from a sense of loss within myself. I am a 'religious person' if that phrase still has meaning; in some sense I believe in God and I am moved to my depths by the meaning I perceive in Christianity. Yet I am saddened by the deadness, the lack of imaginative power and, above all, the self-consciousness, of public religion in Britain, and I am even more saddened by a restlessness and hunger within myself. I recognize the longing for love, the seeking for comfort in food and, less often, in drink, that is so often the mark not simply of my own failure to be fully human, but of a whole society to create simple paths to fulfilment.

The failure is partly in the impersonality of urban society, the way that it is possible to live in a city scarcely knowing, or being known by, other people, and so cut off from simple forms of intimate contact with others that village life supplies. Partly it is a habit of living within the head – the books, the ideas, writing – more than within the natural world. I am much more likely to notice the publication of an interesting new book, for instance, than the arrival of the new moon. This is partly the result of being an urban creature, but it is also because our culture prizes books, ideas, the word, the media, more than it prizes the natural world which is its home. Learning to read taught us how to live in a second world which could then become a substitute for the other. In contrast, a pre-literate people, like the Desert Aborigines, live in constant awareness of the natural world, with the world of myth, mediated in story and song and painting and ceremony, shining through it.

Even physically, it seemed to me, I demonstrated the split between mind and body. The symptom I suffered most from was a headache – I would wake, morning after morning, with a cracking headache rising from my neck to my head. I knew that it came from a particular sort of 'drivenness', my mind and my will overriding the need of my body for laziness, the need to 'sit still'. Everything to be done seemed 'important', 'urgent' – even when I knew that it was not – so that it was hard to stop.

'It's the "chi", the energy,' said a friend who is a T'ai Chi enthusiast, talking about my headaches. 'It gets stuck in your head and neck and cannot travel around your body.' I was irritated by this suggestion, which felt mildly humiliating, mainly because it sounded an uncannily convincing diagnosis. There must be some profound fear in me, I thought, that if I stopped 'doing' I should be dead.

Last year a much-loved friend died of cancer. He had been a religious searcher all his life – it had been one of the powerful links between us – and he had ended a quasi-Buddhist, as I had ended a quasi-Anglican, but he died angrily, furious at having life taken from him, bitterly resentful of those surviving him. It was not hard to see the anger as a mask for fear and, painfully observing his fear of death, I could not fail to recognize my own. Christianity had reached me and healed me at many levels over the years, but did not seem to touch my fear of death. It seemed to me that this had to do with its withdrawal from nature. It did not love the natural world, nor teach its adherents to do so. It was made uneasy by the body, by sexuality and by women, often seen as the visible reminders of sexuality. In contrast, Aborigines saw nature as sacred and relationship with it as the supreme human task.

This interested me because I could remember, in very early childhood, feeling what I can only describe as a 'relationship' with a rose. I stood and gazed at it, moved in and out of it, felt that I was it, and was filled with a wonder which would have been more remarkable if I had been old enough to know that this was not a common feeling. But perhaps at two or three years old it is a common feeling. The rose was sacred, and so was the natural world.

Aldous Huxley describes just such a feeling when he swallowed four tenths of a gram of mescaline and stared at a vase containing a rose, a carnation and an iris. 'I was not looking now at an unusual flower arrangement. I was seeing what Adam had seen on the morning of his creation – the miracle, moment by moment, of naked existence.'[1]

Some years after Huxley's experiment, abetted by a friend who was a psychiatrist, I took LSD and rediscovered the 'miracle of naked existence' by looking at the grain in the table and, then, watching the sun dance on the glass neck of a whisky bottle. So it wasn't just nature in its pure form, I thought, that was caught up into the miracle. All being was the miracle, the Isness or Istigkeit of which Meister Eckhart had spoken.

Slowly, working through painters and poets and novelists and theologians and mystics, and with some help from a psychoanalyst, to whom I shall always be grateful, I tried to approach that miracle. It seemed to me that all my Western conditioning veiled it from me, and made me fearful and suspicious of it. For it is a miracle which, once perceived, makes huge claims. Kowanyama had lifted a corner of the veil, and I guessed that Aborigines were much nearer to the miracle than I was.

I did some searching closer to home. In Cornwall, in Orkney, in Ireland, at Avebury and Silbury and Uffington, at Stonehenge, I had stared in wonder at the great monuments – standing stones, manmade hill, running horse, temple. At the tombs of Newgrange in Ireland and Maes Howe on Orkney – places where, at the winter solstice, the sun shines right into the heart of the tomb and illuminates it – I had marvelled at the integration of religion and astronomy. I had spent hours at the Neolithic house remains of Skara Brae on Orkney, trying to reconstruct for myself a world in which people lived by hunting and gathering – seafood, birds' eggs, birds, wild animals, roots, seeds, plants – and to imagine the weapons and tools used. I thought of how clothes would be made, what dyes would be used to paint the body or to make jewellery or headdresses. I tried to picture their division of labour, the different roles of men and women and children, the tribal sense, the relationships with other tribal groups. I thought about housing, keeping warm, about how people amused themselves and one another. Above all, I thought about what people believed about the meaning of their lives, about the supernatural, about sacredness and about what sense they made of the great questions of identity, of purpose and of death.

When I first began to learn more about Aborigines I thought with excitement that here were living people who might demonstrate some of the answers to my questions. Traditional Aborigines, who were still 'coming in' out of the desert as recently as the 1960s (and one group as late as the 1980s), had lived with as few tools and possessions as any Neolithic man or woman. With a spear, a spearthrower, a boomerang, a digging stick, and a coolamon (a hollowed out piece of tree trunk used as a cradle, water-carrier, or basket) they managed their lives. There were a few favoured items added to this basic set of tools: a belt made out of human hair, useful for tucking things into; sharp stones used as knives; grinding stones with which to turn seeds into flour; ochre, red and yellow, for decorating the body, or sometimes for barter with other tribes; 'dilly' bags, bags made out of fibre, often worn round the neck. But of necessity they travelled light, making temporary camps for themselves with branches and leaves, moving on to the next camp as a new harvest or the promise of fresh meat beckoned. When conditions were favourable they ate well, moving from hunting ground to wild vegetable patch according to the season, finding water often by digging holes – soaks – in dried-up creek beds. In times of drought, as in the terrible years between 1924 and 1930, many died.

It was a life of utter simplicity as far as possessions were concerned, but one of extraordinary richness in the paths of the spirit and of the imagination. The eighteenth-century sailors, soldiers and convicts who burst in upon this secret world, and their nineteenth-century successors – graziers and miners and missionaries and prospectors – had, with rare exceptions, no capacity to understand the value of what they saw. What they thought they saw were 'savages', a projection of their own fear of the unknown.

Most of them understood nothing of the religious belief that fitted the Aboriginal form of life like a skin. They did not know that in this vivid knowledge of a natural world full of sacramental meaning, they were looking through a privileged door to the world of common human ancestors. If there was any awareness of this, it only made the experience more frightening. Indifferent to the fascination of finding a culture that went back to a time before Christianity, Buddhism, Judaism and Islam had imprinted themselves indelibly upon humanity, they could only see barbarians, people who lacked the passwords that made them accepted as equals in the human family. Where the barbarians did not pose an immediate threat in terms of warfare, and many Aborigines fought hard for their territory, they were subjugated, humiliated and exploited by white weaponry and technology. It was not, however, the tragedy, terrible as it was, that drew me to Australia, but a wish to know and understand more of the human reality and the spiritual depth still visible in the peoples of those extraordinary deserts and forests.

I read, and reread Bruce Chatwin's description of the Dreaming in *The Songlines*.

> Each totemic ancestor, while travelling through the country, was thought to have scattered a trail of words and musical notes along the line of his footprints, and . . . these Dreaming-tracks lay over the land as 'ways' of communication between the most far-flung tribes.
>
> 'A song,' Arkady said, 'was both map and direction-finder. Providing you knew the song, you could always find your way across country.'

'And would a man on "Walkabout" always be travelling down one of the Songlines?'

'Yes.'[2]

Chatwin's book about Australia, apart from his interest in the Dreaming, shows surprisingly little general interest in Aboriginal life – his best descriptions mostly concentrate on white Australians – but he drew my attention, as the Australian writer James Cowan was to do later, to the central importance of the land itself.

> The religious life had a single aim: to keep the land the way it was and should be. The man who went 'Walkabout' was making a ritual journey. He trod in the footprints of his Ancestor. He sang the Ancestor's stanzas without changing a word or note – and so recreated the Creation.

With the obsession of passion I continued to seek information, trying, among London's slender Aboriginal pickings, to glean understanding of people at the other end of the world. In Sydney I had once bought a bark painting of an emu, a totem, so it told me on the back, of the Dua moiety. (Sometimes in Aboriginal societies a tribe is divided into two halves – known as moieties – either to share ceremonial responsibilities or to indicate suitable marriage partners.) It was painted in red and yellow ochre and charcoal on flattened stringybark with crosshatching over the bird's wings. The artist was Ray Nungalawi of the language group Maiali, and he came from Manyalaluk, near Katherine in the Northern Territory.

Finding that it was difficult to find the right place for it in my London flat, I had put it away in frustration. Now I got it out again. I tried it in the sitting room where it made everything else – the oil paintings and prints by British artists, the Chinese curtains, even the antique mirror, look faintly ridiculous. Plainly it wouldn't do there. I moved it to the bedroom, but the power from it was too disturbing a presence as I settled down to sleep. Finally, I found just the right place for it between two tall bookshelves – a location not without irony since many Aborigines are pre-literate – in my study where it has hung ever since, buckling ever so slightly in the central heating (bark paintings in art galleries are sheltered within glass cases). The emu and I stared at one another as soon as I opened the door and I slowly began to recognize him as an ally. Because of him, I think, I eventually moved more freely among the magnificent images of Aboriginal art.

Having hung my bark painting I set off to learn more. In an Australian giftshop off the Strand, full of tawdry boomerangs and bits of rather ghastly poker-work, I found a section of secondhand books, among which was M. J. Meggitt's *Desert People*.[3] Meggitt was a student of the anthropologist A. P. Elkin, and was one of the last, between 1953 and 1960, to study an Aboriginal tribe, the Warlbiri, living in its own country and mainly within its own cultural tradition. From Meggitt I learned of the breakdown of tribal organization among Aborigines, hastened, of course, by the white settlers and the missions, but also by the great drought of the 1920s which made life lived alongside whites in many cases a matter of survival. 'They became too much accustomed to the new foods, warm clothes, steel axes and the like to wish to return permanently to the rigorous life of the bush. Everyone now desired these commodities, which could be regularly obtained only as long as some at least of the tribe accepted European employment.'[4]

Were there, I wondered in the late 1980s, people still living as Meggitt had found the Warlbiri in the 1950s? Questions to Australian friends brought uncertain answers. Some were quite sure there still were – in Arnhem Land, in Kakadu, in the Northern Territory, in the Western desert – one was quite sure he knew such a place. Others thought that era was over.

Their answers aroused mixed reactions in me. If I found such people could I cope with such strangeness? (There were, of course, 'tours' which would take me to Kakadu, say, and give me a 'taste' of Aboriginal life while smoothing out the awkwardness for me. Maybe it was snobbery, but the idea made me uneasy. I didn't want to go to inspect Aboriginal life, but to try to be alongside it for a bit. Perhaps it was a fantasy but it was one which appealed to me.)

A few months before I had stood in the British Museum's storehouse in Shoreditch and stared at an assortment of Aboriginal tools and three sacred boards or *tjuringa*, all from what is known in Australia as 'the Western desert', the huge interior desert that is west of the Northern Territory and which runs all the way from the Kimberley

Plateau in the north to the Great Victoria Desert and the Nullabor Plain in the south. At that stage I did not know that uninitiated people were not allowed to look at sacred objects, though I did feel how incongruous it was to be standing in a drab building in London watched by an attendant, examining something its owner had regarded as holy. In just such a judicious way I imagined some man from Mars fingering a crucifix and trying to grasp its arcane meaning. How, I wondered, had the *tjuringas* come into the possession of the British Museum to end in a dusty storehouse? How many hundreds, or thousands, of them did they have hidden away there, few of them ever seeing the light of day (the Museum has no permanent Aboriginal exhibit) unless some researcher such as myself made a special request. These objects, of supreme importance to their original owners, had been whisked away by imperious white men for this dusty death. Well, there is some evidence that *tjuringas* were very occasionally bartered, more usually to other tribes in an exchange of spiritual power. But in this case, I guess it is more likely that Aboriginal people in desperate straits sometimes sold or bartered them for food, or that passing white explorers stole them as souvenirs.

Much later, reading the memoirs of Colonel Egerton Warburton, a British explorer who had helped 'open up' the desert in the 1870s, I found a description of how this could happen, though Colonel Warburton's *tjuringas* never made it as far as the British Museum.

> Found two stone slabs marked, and a round stone hidden in a hole on the top of the hill; brought them away as curiosities. These slabs were thin, flat stones measuring about fifteen inches by six, of an oblong shape and rounded at the ends. They were marked with unintelligible scrawls, and were secreted in a hole when I pulled them out in company with a spherical stone about the size of an orange. No clue could be gained as to what they meant, or why they were deposited there. Unfortunately these interesting objects had to be thrown away before the termination of the journey.

The *tjuringas* I saw in the British Museum were objects of great beauty. The smaller one, in red mulga wood, was inscribed in a

21

pattern of joined concentric circles. The bigger one, in stone, had a minimal circular pattern.

The other objects I had asked to see were also good to look at: a boomerang, a spearthrower or woomera, some flint tools, very like the ones it is still possible to find in the Weald, a piece of sharpened stone used, it was claimed, for circumcision, and a knife in which a shard of bottle glass was fastened to a handle with gum and string. This last artefact, though some fifty years old, showed the way Aboriginal people had taken an object from the white world and adapted it to their own needs.

My original fascination with Australian Aboriginal people had come to me entirely by chance. On a visit to New South Wales in 1984 to give some lectures I had met a clergyman's wife, Joy, who happened to be a house guest with the family where I was staying. She and her husband Philip, an Anglican priest, lived at the Aboriginal settlement of Kowanyama, on the Mitchell river, in north Queensland, near the Gulf of Carpentaria. Over breakfast Joy began to talk to me about Aborigines whom hitherto I had only noticed as dark ghosts on the fringes of large Australian towns. When I had asked local white Australians about them I had heard a long catalogue about shiftlessness and drinking, about a Government supposedly lavish with money in an attempt to solve a problem that was intractable. Joy's conversation was quite different. About a thousand Aborigines lived at Kowanyama, the remnant of three different tribes.

'At the turn of the century, graziers were beginning to take up land on the Cape York Peninsula, and the local Aborigines were driven out. In some cases they were poisoned or shot. The Anglican church set up a school, hospital and church at Kowanyama, and gradually what was left of the three tribes of Cape York came and settled there.'

This story moved me, as many stories about the dispossession of Aborigines were to do, I think because of the sense of the destruction of innocence. A trusting people who asked little except to live on their traditional lands, picking the plants and hunting the animals they needed in order to stay alive, had their trust destroyed as they became themselves the hunted. Like Adam and Eve they were cast out of Eden.

I asked questions. Eventually, Joy said, 'If you can ever spare the time, why not come and stay?'

The following year, returning to Australia to give some more lectures, I took her up on the offer. I arrived by aeroplane – it was impossible to reach Kowanyama overland during the Wet or for some weeks afterwards because the fragile tracks of mud and sand were washed away. It was tropical country and I had not really been prepared for that. Kowanyama stood on the banks of a magnificent river lined with cabbage palm trees. Innumerable white corella birds sat in the branches looking like giant magnolia blossoms. Apart from Kowanyama itself there were no towns, no villages, no roads, no people, only bush and antbeds and vast, slow, brown rivers where an occasional alligator surfaced.

In addition to its school and church (the hospital had closed in the era of flying doctors and helicopter lifts for emergency cases), Kowanyama had many Government-built houses, a great barn of a hall and social centre, a store, an outdoor arena for games, the inevitable airstrip and a lock-up, mainly used to keep drunks out of harm's way. There was almost no employment.

Although there were no people in the bush there were plenty of creatures – wallabies, wild turkeys, wild pigs – who used to appear from behind bushes, or rush across the roads. The wild turkeys, taken by surprise, have a wonderfully lewd call, 'Oooo!'

At Kowanyama I went 'hunting' with a rather elderly group from the church. We stopped at the first creek we came to and the women got down with their digging sticks and speared a few crabs to take home for supper. We drove on across the bush and found a beautiful open site for our picnic on the shores of a wide shallow river.

'This is our country,' one of the women told me, 'very special. On other side of river, very evil.' The other side of the river looked similar to our side, and I pondered her words. It reminded me of a terror of certain places I had experienced as a child, and might experience still if

I did not sternly tell myself it was nonsense. (Later I remembered feeling it as an adult on a visit to the Tower.) Inside that terror it feels as if certain places have soaked up horror and are impregnated with it.

The women made a campfire and began baking potatoes and making tea in a billy. One of them was making damper with some flour she had brought with her. About fifty yards away the men had made a fire and over it they were singeing the hair from a wallaby they had killed. Blackened, it made an unexpectedly awesome sight, partly because, like all kangaroos, it had an unnervingly human look. The oldest Aborigine, a slender, handsome old man with a magnificent white beard and head of white hair, was teaching Philip a ritual way to cook the wallaby – 'Murrie style' as he called it. The fire, having got going, was damped down to embers, the wallaby's body was laid upon the embers, filled with hot stones, and covered with cabbage palm leaves and sand. There it was left for several hours.

Meanwhile, I went walking with some of the women who wanted to show me 'their country', and I was touched by their care for me. When I tripped and fell over a root, however, there was a good deal of amusement. It was definitely their sort of joke. When we got back Philip announced we were all going swimming in the river. The thought of the cool water was welcome but I had no bathing suit. Would they mind if I bathed naked?

'We bathe wearing our clothes,' said Philip, and so we did, letting the sun and the heat of our bodies dry our shirts and trousers. It was a lovely way to keep cool but I guess it showed how the prudishness of past generations of missionaries had passed physical selfconsciousness on to the Aborigines. By now the potatoes and tea and damper were on the go, and later on we moved over to the men's fire (or camp as the Aborigines called it) and tasted the wallaby.

We bumped home exhausted in the back of the truck, covered, as usual, in dust from the dried-up road.

Philip and Joy only had a small house in which they lived with two small sons. I slept in a caravan in the garden. I was often disturbed at night by the cattle which roamed the whole area and could be heard lowing at all hours. One night, however, I heard what was evidently a bull bellowing furiously only a few feet away from where I was lying in bed. I pictured a pair of sharp horns bursting through the thin wall of the caravan and impaling me and I hastily got up. The bellowing went on for an hour or more but nothing else happened.

One quite small thing made a much greater impression on me, though. It was the sight of an old Aboriginal man sitting absolutely still on the grass outside the church for maybe an hour, waiting for the service to begin. He did not fidget, nor chatter, nor show any impatience, but sat, in total relaxation, a sort of collectedness. I was not sure that I had seen that sort of stillness in a human being, or at least not for a long time. I wanted to understand the secret of it, I who have such difficulty with sitting still, always scheming and planning and thinking of things to do. It started in me a kind of hunger for what these people had, and it was all the more remarkable since in many ways they had suffered terrible hardships.

There was May, for instance. She, a woman in her fifties, was a child of mixed white and Aboriginal blood, and like many, many other Aboriginal, or half-Aboriginal children, was taken away from her natural parents and brought up in white surroundings. The bizarre belief had been that, if a child had any white blood in it, it deserved a white upbringing. The misery, anguish and despair this brought to many Aboriginal mothers was ignored. Learning that 'the officer' was on his way round collecting partly white children, they would blacken their children's skins to conceal their white genes.

I was deeply shocked to learn of the forcible removal of children – it seemed to have a Nazi brutality about it – but gradually learned it had happened on an enormous scale. Not only mixed-race children were removed, nor did the horror end, as is sometimes claimed, in the 1940s. A social worker in Perth in 1993 told me that to this day she repeatedly meets young Aboriginal women in their twenties who were taken from their natural parents, usually without their consent, and brought up virtually as servants, or, worse, as 'children' expected to give sexual favours to their supposed father.

I was saddened too by the endemic unemployment at Kowanyama, at the sight of a huge community of people with nothing to do, living largely off welfare. Drinking and gambling, inevitably, became ways of passing the long days.

Then, and later, I was curious about the role of missions in the Aboriginal saga. In the nineteenth and twentieth centuries as Australia opened up and graziers, miners, pearlers and others began to make use of Aboriginal labour, the missions alone had no economic axe to grind. Frequently, they took up the role of defending Aborigines against exploitation, of protesting at acts of violence against them, or at legal sanctions which caused them terrible suffering. In times of starvation and drought they fed as many as could make their way to them out of the desert.

Of course, a price was exacted. Many of the missions, though by no means all, saw the Aborigines as crude heathen, with a religion for which they had scant regard. Missionaries tended to believe in clothes, regular hours and discipline, all notions completely alien to nomadic peoples in a hot country. Taking the food and other precious things the missions offered, the Aborigines naturally absorbed religious imagery and ideas as well. They do not seem to have been reluctant to do this, in so far as they understood all that was being offered. It was rather that, being deeply religious people, they absorbed the undoubted faith of their new teachers, and added it on to their own religious experience. If they had to, they put up with the discipline, and what they probably saw as the oddities, of their mentors. They learned what it suited them to learn. Later developments suggest that it may have been less than the devoted missionaries believed at the time.

Philip, the Anglican priest at Kowanyama, typified a younger generation of missionary with a very different idea of the task. He saw himself as there not to convert, but to give some sort of reparation to people who had been badly hurt by white intervention in their country and way of life. Watching him, rather than listening to him say it, I saw that he felt a need to learn from the people he worked amongst. I still see him patiently preparing the body of the wallaby 'Murrie style' with the old man carefully instructing him as he did so.

He was loved for this approach, and given a 'skin name' – that is to say he was adopted as a relative by an Aboriginal family. Listening to him, I began to struggle with the hugely complex network of Aboriginal relationships, a network I still only partly understand. Mothers-in-law, or others who stood in the relation of mothers-in-law, as some of the women at Kowanyama now did to Philip, could not publicly recognize their sons-in-law or be recognized by them, though the sons-in-law had some obligation to make sure that they did not want for the necessities of life. The two might not sit in a room together, and if they saw the other approaching on the ròad, were obliged to turn aside.

A fairly small number of Aborigines came to Philip's church, though probably no fewer than would attend in an English parish. A service was held daily at eleven o'clock and, anything up to an hour beforehand, the worshippers would start arriving and would sit, very often silent and still, on the grass outside the church. The beginning of the service was not necessarily a signal for anyone to get up and enter the church, but gradually over the next quarter of an hour they would do so. What remains with me about the services was the extraordinary singing – deep, rich, sepulchral singing, unlike any sound I had ever heard before. It took me a while to realize that the hymns were ones well known to me. The peculiar style of drawing out the words and the music, the unusual pronunciation of English, transformed them into something quite different.

The service over, Philip would serve tea and his congregation would drink it, exchange a little conversation, sit for a while on the grass again, and then, anything up to an hour later, stroll gently home. There was never any sense of hurry.

One night, Philip was woken to go down to the church because somebody had been heard moving around inside it, and there was a certain amount of concern that it might be a ghost. Feeling a little nervous himself he went in and found a young man known to him who poured out a heart-rending story. They had had a dance that night in the hall and, needing money, he had stolen the takings. But then guilt had assailed him and he had had a unique idea about how to relieve it. He had decided to break into the church and give himself sacramental wine as a form of absolution, and it was in this act that Philip found him.

This introduction to an Aboriginal community made me long to find one less fragmented. I did not underestimate the problems. I was a Pom, for a start, dyed in the wool of an imperial past, however much I might try to disclaim it. Whereas I was more or less welcome among white Australians, they often made it clear that as a Pom I could know and understand nothing of Aboriginal Australians. Some suggested that it would be a mistake to try. I might have paid more attention if more of them had shown firsthand knowledge themselves.

So far as the Aborigines themselves were concerned I came to understand, much later, that being a woman was an even more ineradicable problem than being white. Theoretically, it was possible for white men to undergo Aboriginal initiation ceremonies and become one with Aboriginal men, privy to their deepest secrets. I was to meet a white photographer at Balgo, his body covered in scars as if he had been severely beaten, who had done just that. I did not ask him whether he had been circumcised or subincised but the chances are he had been. That was how initiation took place in that part of Australia. As a woman, however, I was excluded from both the pain and from the deepest secrets.

Then there was the problem of language. Traditional Aborigines, unlike their urban brothers and sisters, speak mainly in their own language, and often in several other local languages as well. Eloquent in their own tongue, and good linguists, in English they speak haltingly and often in a 'pidgin' or 'Kriol' style that is difficult to follow and debases the sentiments it tries to express. It was the language of 'servants' and 'hands', domestics and cattlemen – it is not the speech of free people with important things to say. If I could spend several years in an Aboriginal community, I felt I might become fluent in the local language but most of my life was in England. If I was to learn more about traditional life, that meant being forced back upon interpretation, not just of language, but also of incomprehensible ideas, and interpretation meant the presence of other white people. I also needed other white people, I knew, as a 'passport' into the black Aboriginal world. Aborigines had scant reason to trust white people, unless they approached them through other white people they already trusted. My experience at Kowanyama made me feel that a mission was probably the best approach. I knew the dubious past of some missions, and the scorn with which they are regarded by some Aborigines, and even more by radical white writers – for example, John Pilger in *A Secret Country* (1989)[5] – yet on the whole I trusted the non-fanatical type of missionary more than I trusted the subversive writers. They knew and often cared more, and had less of a sensational axe to grind. Enquiries, this time in Catholic circles, led me to Balgo Hills in the

Great Sandy Desert. This seemed to be exactly what I was looking for. Just as I was about to make my final travel arrangements a warning letter came from Sister Adele, one of the Balgo Sisters of Mercy who ran a clinic there.

> The problem of alcohol has reached a dangerous stage at Balgo over the last three months. Days pass quietly and then a sudden burst of violence will result in damaged buildings, windows, cars and threats in some instances to non-Aboriginal people. Without the problems produced by alcohol, the people here are peaceful and friendly. However, the reality is that much of this year Balgo has been characterized by violence and trouble or 'humbug', as people say here. Realizing the difficulty of the situation I am writing now to let you know that the Sisters in Balgo wanted to convey to you that they do not think it would be wise to be in Balgo for an extended period of time.

I let some time pass, and by then the alcohol epidemic seemed to have blown over.

There was another, more personal and more embarrassing, problem that troubled me more in prospect than the thought of the effects of alcohol. Throughout my time at Kowanyama I had noticed a deep and uncontrollable shyness in myself as I began to meet Aborigines. At home I am talkative and reasonably at ease in social situations but, at Kowanyama, I found myself unnervingly tongue-tied. Partly it was that the usual lubricants of social meeting were removed. There was no small talk, no shared background, in a sense nothing to say that wasn't a question, and I knew that firing out questions wouldn't be the right thing to do either. Aborigines at Kowanyama felt none of my Western sense of obligation that one 'ought' to talk. They felt no more compulsion in this direction than they felt about time, but I was as unaccustomed to social silence as I was to not worrying about time, and I was hugely, ridiculously, ill at ease. I never entirely overcame this, though on the hunting day I remember feeling for the first time as natural a part of the landscape as an outsider had any right to feel.

All the same my shyness had frightened me. It suggested a gulf between people – that is, between myself and Aborigines – that I did not want to acknowledge. I wanted some sort of closeness, acknowledged understanding, warmth, and had no idea if I could manage it even if others could. The spectre of 'difference' which, unacknowledged, lies at the root of racial problems, haunted me. I was more racist than I knew, or wanted to know, and this was a source of secret shame and fear in me. Yet, nevertheless, I was drawn.

CHAPTER THREE

Biddy and I are sitting up beside the driver in the front of a truck, trying to talk about our families – two women with a lot of life behind them speaking of what has mattered most to them. Biddy has a wise old face, lined by experience and by continual exposure to brilliant sun. She wears a T-shirt and a flowery skirt and I feel her body, shapeless but strong, squashed against mine as the driver negotiates the track out of the camp.

'How many children?' asks Biddy.

'Two,' I say. 'A girl and a boy.'

'How big?'

'Very big. Grown up.'

'Grandchildren?'

'Not yet,' I say.

'I have six,' says Biddy. 'Have you father, mother?'

'Mother finished, father finished,' I say, knowing this is one of the local euphemisms for death, a word that is hard to speak.

'You cry?' asks Biddy, and makes a motion of tears running down the cheeks. I realize that I don't. It seems a long time now since my parents died, and though I wish now and again I could tell them things, or share a joke with my father, I suspect I don't feel the grief Biddy is talking about. But I nod.

The endlessness of the desert stretches out behind us and before us: the Great Sandy Desert to the south and north, the Tanami Desert to the east, the Kearney range of mountains in the middle distance, the Lewis range far away. Thirteen hours steady driving down 'the

Tanami', one of the few major highways, would get us to Alice Springs. But south of us, and more important to us, is the huge sweep of 'Kukatja country' between Thomas Peak and Lake Dennis, in the west and east, Emily Springs and Lake Lucas. To the west of Kukatja country is Walmajarri country, and between Kukatja and Walmajarri have been friendly relations and intermarriage. Nowadays many Walmajarri live at Balgo, as well as many Jaru. Other peoples liked the Kukatja less. The Central Desert Aranda used to sneer at the Kukatja for having long, ugly penises, a sneer that was a prelude, I imagine, to picking a serious row.

'Where you from?' Biddy asks me.

'England,' I answer.

'Long way.'

'Yes, a long way.'

'Aeroplane?' she asks, and I nod again.

'I've been in jetplane,' she tells me. 'To Canberra.'

'Why?' I ask.

'To dance,' she tells me. I learned later that some of the women had danced at the World Council of Churches Meeting at Canberra in 1990, a source of pride to Biddy, yet a minor tragedy in itself. The Aboriginal women are accustomed to spend hours over their dancing, slowly working themselves to the climax of the dance. The 'white' timetable of the WCC had no understanding of this and expected them to have finished at the end of the allotted time. Naturally, they were just getting going at that point, and carried on dancing. So eventually they were stopped in order to make way for the next item and remained hurt and angry at this wounding interruption.

Like the well-meaning white organizers I feel myself capable of terrible gaffes, but Biddy, like most Aboriginal women I have met, was good at giving me clues and signals if I was alert enough to notice them. I soon discovered the need to unlearn some of my own social conditioning: to remember not to stare into people's eyes when I first met them, but to lower my eyes so that they would not feel 'shame'. When I shook hands I should not ask people's names – though it is in order to ask another person to inform you about the first person, I should not pepper someone with questions, and I should give them lots of time to think out the answer to a question. I needed to remember that there are social *tabus* that I didn't understand and never would, for example, that there are people who may not speak to one another, as already mentioned, or even be in the same room together. There is a euphemism for this among Aborigines – 'there is no room' – which may puzzle the *kartiya* (white people) looking at a virtually empty room, but the clue must be picked up.

The most central and important idea seemed to be that of 'shame' or rather the avoidance of it. It extends to not rebuking a child in school in front of its fellows, or doing anything at all that makes another feel uncomfortable or awkward. It shows, it seemed to me, an extraordinary delicacy of manners and a great deal of commonsense about the difficulties of human intercourse. Western social life makes the impossible demand upon us that we appear confident and at ease with people we are meeting for the first time. Few of us do feel entirely confident, so we learn to pretend, and not to be very sensitive to our own and others' feeling of 'shame'. And how we plague one another with questions!

I wonder if we let ourselves know all our feelings about colour or any kind of physical difference from ourselves. In the earliest human communities, our very survival may have depended on learning to remark the characteristics of people genetically like ourselves, and on remembering to be suspicious of those who did not look like us. It was only relatively late in human history that different races began to mix, and this process has speeded up tremendously in the last two centuries.

It would not be surprising if we still retained some of our earlier tendency to be suspicious of people who do not look like us, and there is all too much evidence that we are still influenced by this very primitive reaction. We need both to notice the primitive reaction and, then, realize how inappropriate to our present lives is this crude sense that anyone who does not look like us is an 'enemy' and is, conveniently, somewhat less human than we are. And so to the slippery slide to persecution and genocide.

Political correctness makes it difficult to admit to the kind of shock another person's colour can induce at first sight. For the first few days at Balgo I was endlessly surprised at *how* black people were, and I observed that it was a different black from that of the West Indians I know and am used to at home in North Kensington. Bruce Chatwin observed rightly that Aborigines are 'matt black', not 'glitter black' like Negroes. I was surprised too that many of the children had blonde or tawny-coloured hair, in striking contrast to their dark bodies. I thought at first this must be due to mixed blood but discovered, later, that there is a Pintupi gene which yields fair or tawny hair, and that the Kukatja are related to the Pintupi.

Then there was something I might describe as the 'fierceness' of the men. Some of them, not all, had a warrior-like look that made me feel I would hate to offend them. I suspect, with my own quality of 'shame', that it had something to do with their similarity to the traditional stereotype of the savage.

With the possible exception of the Mojave desert, I am not sure that I have ever stayed in a place that had as much physical or psychological impact on me as Balgo. Heat, glare and wind (the name Balgo – *Parlku* in Kukatja – means 'dirty wind') made it physically taxing, but I soon learnt to accommodate to those. Other things affected me more profoundly. The brilliant redness of the ground, the oceanic sweep of the desert, the vast sunsets and the elf-light that preceded the dawn, soon began to appear in my dreams, as they still do, as if I was caught up in the meditation of God.

The dreams were usually of the desert itself or of the red space at the centre of the settlement which they call 'the Oval'. The main buildings of Balgo were grouped around it. There was the modest church with its steeple, and the priests' house alongside it, both of them built in a red stone. The priests' house had a kitchen and a community room, nearly always empty. This led into a corridor, a sort of cloister, open down one side, but with heavy iron mesh filling in the gap. The visitors' bedrooms opened off this cloister, and the cloister itself was useful to hang washing (it dried like lightning in the hot dry air) or for just sitting in the cool.

In front of the house was a little grass and a few ghost gum trees, their white trunks gleaming in the half light of dawn and dusk. Moving round the Oval there was the one-storey school, the adult education centre, the art centre, the clinic (where in the hot weather people made excuses to come 'For cool, Sistah, for cool!') and houses where a number of the teachers lived. In one corner was the big hangar of 'the store'. Behind were the three Aboriginal camps, that is clusters of prefab houses built with Government money, a number of them with solar heating. Cruelly hot for much of the year, sometimes over 50°C, in the cold season Balgo can be chilly, especially at night. There were a very few of the old humpy type of house, but a few traditional lean-tos, belonging either to those who preferred to sleep out of doors in the heat, or those who still chose to live in traditional style. There were also the two Law camps – the men's and the women's – places of ritual observance where white people, or Aborigines of the opposite sex, were not allowed to go.

The absolute simplicity of the place stays with me – there was virtually nothing there that was not regularly needed, no urban luxuries. I had a recurring fantasy of starting an ice cream parlour.

All around Balgo was desert, with no sign of human habitation. The nearest town, Hall's Creek, was 260 kilometres away by sandy track – a track which usually got washed away in the Wet, making the journey hazardous. To go anywhere by car or track around Balgo was to invite punctures, to risk getting water in the engine from driving through flooded creeks, shooting off the road by accident, or 'rolling', or to suffer the much worse danger of getting lost. There were terrible stories of people, sometimes with children, who set off across the desert in a faulty truck and without enough water or petrol, who were found dead. It was not unusual, particularly around the time of the Wet, for Balgo to house refugees from floods, or people who had broken down or got lost. Government workers needing to visit often felt the need to bring a companion with them on the heroic journey by car. One welfare worker, while I was there, persuaded a friend to fly her in by aeroplane.

*

Having necessarily arrived at Balgo with the weekly mail, I was dropped complete with mailbag at the priests' house where, like all visitors, I would stay.

Until the 1980s, Balgo was a Catholic Mission but then, under federal rules, the Church formally handed the place over to the Aboriginal community and stayed on at their invitation to work in the clinic, the school and the outstations – Billiluna, Mularn and Yagga Yagga. The place was now officially called Wirrumanu – a beautiful name, I thought, which derives from the *luurnpa* or kingfisher who is a totemic ancestor of the Kukatja. Wirrumanu is the dreaming journey or flight of the *luurnpa*. From habit, though, everyone seemed to continue to talk about Balgo or Balgo Hills.

'Hooray! The bright spot of the week,' remarked Robin, one of the two Jesuit priests who minister at Balgo. He meant the mail, not me. He relinquished the sack regretfully and took me to see my room. I was pleased that it included a kitchen, shower and lavatory, and a shelf where I could put my books, files and laptop. Best of all it had a fan and an airconditioner.

Robin was a good-looking man in his thirties with a black beard and strong profile. He had only recently completed his Jesuit studies in Melbourne, and was still getting used to the simplicities of life in the bush. He had spent the last year at the Aboriginal centre at Port Keats, and had come to Balgo to a permanent job three months previously. His major task was to learn the local language.

'It's mainly Kukatja people here, but there are also some Walmajarri and Jaru. Kukatja is the main language spoken, though most people here speak three or more local languages, as well as some English. I am trying to learn Kukatja.'

'Is it difficult?'

'The main problem is getting relationships right. The grammar alters according to how many people you are speaking to and what your relationship to them is.'

The conversation was interrupted by one of the nursing sisters, Anita, a warm, forthright woman who, I was later to learn, seemed ready to tackle anything or anyone. On this occasion, she was in obvious distress. I would have left tactfully but the tea was only just being poured.

'The baby died,' she said. One of the Balgo babies had been bitten by a mosquito carrying Ross River virus, had developed meningitis, and had died that morning. The two of them discussed funeral arrangements, while I looked about with some curiosity. On the dresser was a folded stole, a pyx and a missal. In the corner were a couple of guitars and in another corner stood a *nulla-nulla*, a big red stick.

When Anita had gone Robin told me about the history of Balgo. The Catholic Church, in the guise of several different religious orders, had an association with the Kukatja that went back to the 1940s.

'Was the point to convert them?'

'I don't think so. The first intention was to set up a leprosarium – Hansen's disease was rampant among the desert Aborigines. That fell through from lack of funds and Government support. Then there was the attempt to provide decent living and working conditions. Missionaries in those days were terribly tough – much tougher than I am – and they set up cattle stations, which I wouldn't begin to know how to do, so that people had work.'

'So did the Aborigines on the Mission become Catholic?'

'Eventually many did, though to begin with the Fathers in charge discouraged adult baptism, I think because they had a lot of respect for Aboriginal beliefs. Aborigines are very religious people, and they are good at seeing what religion is about. In a sense they just added Catholic belief on to their other beliefs. It didn't replace them, it just got added on.'

That night I dined with the Sisters. Although they only lived just across the Oval one of them came and collected me by truck. Night journeys by foot involved the careful use of a flashlight to avoid the danger of stepping on a snake. The Sisters' house, one of a common Australian design made from a prefabricated kit, was inside a sort of wire cage, with big gates that could be locked at night. I was struck by the need for security at Balgo – by the iron mesh on the priests' house and the kind of 'compound' security of the Sisters'. It reminded me of that earlier letter with its mention of drink and violence.

The Sisters' front door opened into a dining room with a sideboard and table, and leading from the dining room was the kitchen. On the other side of the dining room a door led into the sitting room where armchairs were ranged around a television set and a rather inferior Aboriginal painting hung on the wall. Another corridor led to the bedrooms. To enter this house was to step out of the timeless world of Balgo and into suburbia. Later I came to see just why the Sisters might crave a little suburban security, but at first the house was a shock.

As for clothes, I saw at once that my style of jeans or shorts, shirts, desert boots or plimsolls, and Akubra hat were out of order. The Sisters wore cotton summer dresses or skirts in the Laura Ashley tradition, usually with rather pretty sandals and straw hats. I had not brought a single skirt with me. (I soon discovered that the Aboriginal women never seemed to wear trousers either, preferring a cotton dress or a skirt and T-shirt. I suspect that the underlying dress code of Balgo was that men were men and women were women, but I never dared to ask in case I should feel humiliated by my wardrobe.)

The Sisters of Mercy covered quite a wide age-range. Marie and Margaret taught in Luurnpa School, Cecilia in the Adult Education Centre. Mary Jane, Joan and Carmel were nurses, who worked in the Balgo Clinic and in and out of people's homes as was necessary. They were helped by Cheryl and Anita who belonged to a Catholic lay order of nurses who devoted their lives to working for the needy, and Margaret, a nurse who had come to work there for the adventure.

'What are the health problems?'

'Mainly those brought about by malnutrition – diabetes, heart disease, skin problems,' Sister Mary Jane told me. 'There are a lot of eye and ear problems too. Boils, sores, scabies, lice.' She went on to explain that nowadays nobody gave birth at Balgo. Two weeks before the birth they were flown into hospital in Broome. Balgo and its outstations also made regular use of the Flying Doctor service. Mary Jane had an enchanting giggle and a spontaneous gaiety, like a teenager for whom life is still new and untried. It was a shock, therefore, to hear her discussing the best treatment for spear wounds with one of the other sisters.

'Spear wounds?' I said, appalled.

'Yes, there are fights, sometimes with spears, sometimes with boomerangs, and we have to deal with the wounds. The first thing's to stop the bleeding. There's another sort of spear wound, too. If a man breaks the Law [she meant the Aboriginal Law, the social and ritualistic rules that govern traditional Aborigines] he may have a spear put through his thigh. They do it in such a way that it does not cause lasting injury, but it incapacitates him at the time, and it is agony.'

'What sort of thing would he have had to have done to be punished like that?'

'Well, for example, if he married a woman not of the right "skin".'

'And what would happen to him after that?'

'That would be that. The good thing about their punishments is that once they are over they are over. There are no further recriminations.'

Some other fights were due to alcohol. Balgo was officially 'dry', but now and again a truck would come up from Alice with 'grog' on board and some of the Balgo men would get drunk and get into fights. I remembered Adele's warning letter.

'They say it takes seven generations for the enzymes in the human body to learn to deal with alcohol,' Sister Joan told me. 'It's all right for us with our generations of Irish ancestors [nearly all the Sisters did seem to have at least some Irish blood], but the Aborigines are still new to it.'

The Adult Education Centre offered teaching in literacy, cooking, sewing, handicrafts and other interests. A handful of adults qualified to train as teachers or to go to technical colleges.

'Come and have a look if you'd like to. Tomorrow afternoon?'

Sister Cecilia, who taught there, had only recently come to Balgo but already had been given a 'skin' relationship with an Aboriginal family.

The Sisters of Mercy is a huge order in Australia and there are differences between the various sections of it. Sister Joan said that her 'mob', in addition to the usual vows of poverty, chastity and obedience, took a fourth vow 'to serve the poor'. One Sister remarked that some Sisters did not work with the poor at all, but with well-to-do people, for instance, in fairly posh girls' schools.

'Well, the rich often need help as much as the poor,' someone remarked.

I remarked that the rich had more choices than the poor, were not so helpless. No one seemed to agree with this.

Before I went home, Sister Joan thoughtfully found a fly net for me to borrow which would fit over my Akubra hat and protect my face. I had been in Balgo long enough to be very grateful. Flies settling upon hands and arms were irritating, but easily waved away. There was something about them settling in clouds on one's face, and particularly near to the eyes, that I found intolerable. It was also easy to swallow one, particularly if one was speaking. Sometimes, wearing a net, so many settled upon it, that it was difficult to see out.

I walked home across the sand. The stars were clear and beautiful, and I could hear cicadas or tree frogs singing, I wasn't sure which. But I was too busy watching the ground to appreciate the night properly, anxiously shining my torch to avoid the peculiar horror of stepping on a snake. As I entered my room a tiny lizard shot through the door ahead of me. I like lizards, but could not help wondering nervously whether it would run over me in the night. Why would it matter, I asked myself, that this harmless, pretty creature should touch me with its little feet?

As I undressed I heard a strange human cry, of pain, of desolation. I put a blanket over my shoulders and went out into the cloister to listen. The sound came from a long way off, and I was not even sure of the direction.

CHAPTER FOUR

There was a time, perhaps two million years ago, when the vast continent of Australia was almost empty of creatures, both human and animal. Marsupials were the only animals to flourish. Bats, mice and rats were the first placental land mammals to cross the sea from the Indonesian islands. They arrived in New Guinea and Australia long before human beings.

In the period of the Ice Age or Pleistocene epoch – which began about 1.6 million years ago – archaic humans, collectively known as *homo erectus*, began to move out of Africa and into southern Eurasia. One million or so years ago they had reached south-east Asia, notably Java. In what is thought to have been the first sea voyage in human history, their descendant, *homo sapiens*, the ancestor of the modern Australian Aborigines and Melanesians, crossed the straits dividing Australia from Asia. This first voyage may have accomplished much more than the explorers expected in bringing them to a new land, but multiple voyages succeeded it, bringing a wide diversity of languages and genes and, at a later stage, dingo dogs. In simple boats, probably designed for fishing or for short journeys between islands, the voyagers travelled as much as 150 kilometres.

There is evidence that they occupied Australia forty or fifty thousand years ago. By 30,000 BC there were people at Lake Mungo in south-eastern Australia. Ten thousand years later they were living in the region that is now Sydney Harbour, scratching pictures in caves on the Nullarbor Plain. Middens, flint chips and bone points reveal that two millennia later they were in nearly every habitable

41

part of the Australian continent. In the words of Robert Hughes, 'a membrane of human culture had been stretched over the vast terrain'.[1]

Tough and resourceful, these first inhabitants adapted to the many different countrysides in which they found themselves. In the east or the south or the tropical north, they lived in country generous with fish, game and water. In the centre and to the west was desert, in places a desert of unforgiving harshness, yet here too they adapted with skill and hard work and extraordinary ingenuity. Their task was both simple and vital: they had to find food and water, whatever the climate or season; they had to find covering appropriate to their needs; they had to build shelter which would protect them, their old people and their babies from heat or rain. They were like us, since human needs have a way of always being the same, and they were unlike us in their absolute poverty and simplicity. They owned nothing but a few tools – sticks, spears, carved tree trunks, human hair. Inevitably, they were close to nature in a way we can scarcely imagine, intimately involved in weather changes, the presence or absence of water, the growth of plants, the running of animals, the sight of the stars and the moon.

Like all human beings they lived with, or maybe I mean on, stories. They believed in a heroic, sacred time, long long ago, when the world came to be as it was. To this period two of the earliest writers about Aboriginal culture, Spencer and Gillen, gave the name 'the Dreaming' or 'the Dreamtime' and this has come to be widely accepted by white people and by Aborigines trying to help white people to understand. Aboriginal groups sometimes have slightly different words for it, as in the Aranda expression 'the men of old'. The Kukatja word for 'the Dreaming' is *tjukurrpa*.

Before the Dreaming the world was flat, formless, without features. Then, in sacred time, Dreaming time, the 'Men of Old' or 'the Ancestors' (most of whom were animals or interchangeably animal and human) lived lives of incident, travelling great distances, fighting, feeling lust and jealousy, having sex, urinating, sleeping, menstruating, giving birth, cheating one another, enjoying themselves. All these utterly human incidents marked the landscape for good – colouring it or shaping it or denting it or filling it with water – because the actors had divine status. Finally the landscape became set in its finished sacred form. The framework had become fixed, but the sacredness continued and needed to be remembered (if that is the word for a truth that is felt to be existing now) and maintained in ceremonies which continued to celebrate the awesomeness of the natural world.

For thousands of years the Aborigines were peoples who lived with a sense of clan order, attending large group gatherings in season to practise initiation ceremonies and to share in 'increase rituals' together. They had a sophisticated sense both of how to settle local disputes and avoid overall tyranny, something that Europe, for example, never quite achieved. Some Aboriginal local clans were on friendly terms with neighbours, and exchanged important tokens such as ochre or sacred boards, or intermarried. Others were traditional enemies and fought against each other from time to time. But, perhaps because mutual claims on the natural world were modest, and because, even out in the deserts, most managed to survive and even survive quite well, Aboriginal culture seems to have enjoyed a dignified and reasonably peaceable history.

I am talking about something very like a high civilization, peoples with powerful and satisfying myths, respected rituals, stable political systems, and reasonable protection and consideration for all. In the realm of art, the magnificent Obiri cave paintings on the East Alligator River, which predate the art of Pharaoh's Egypt by 20,000 years, or the Wandjina cave paintings of north west Kimberley, show the ability and the spiritual depth of Aboriginal painters and are now thought to be among the most significant early paintings in the world. Art, as always in its origins, is tied into ceremonial or mythical ideas. As the sacred stories were sung or told, totemic creatures were painted in ochre on bark or upon cave walls or, in desert areas, upon the sand itself.

Then a very different culture slowly approached the closed and settled Aboriginal world. In 1606 a Dutch sea-captain, William Jansz, put ashore at the Gulf of Carpentaria, that sharp tropical spike at the top of northern Australia. There was an unpleasant encounter with some local Aborigines and a Dutch sailor was killed. In 1623 another Dutchman, Jan Cartstenz, captured an Aboriginal prisoner and carried him off to Batavia. Cartstenz didn't care for his glimpse of Australia and its people and claimed to find both the country and its inhabitants the most depressing and miserable on earth. In 1628, G. F. De Witt commented on the 'wild, black and barbaric inhabitants' of the Kimberley.

The English pirate, William Dampier, who beached in King Sound for repairs in 1688, also disliked both the country and its inhabitants, asserting that the people were ape-like and half-blind because of the flies.

Abel Tasman discovered what is now Tasmania in 1642. He was followed by Captain Cook who, sailing into Botany Bay in April 1770, was surprised by how very different Australia had appeared from the lusher New Zealand he had recently left. Despite hostility from the local Aborigines, Cook admired and appreciated what he saw – a people who cared little for material things and preserved a dignity in the face of the modest invasion of the *Endeavour*.

Cook contradicted Dampier's negative verdict. 'They may appear to some to be the most wretched people on earth, but in reality they are far happier than we Europeans, being wholly unacquainted not only with the superfluous but the necessary Conveniences so much sought after in Europe, they are happy in not knowing the use of them. They live in Tranquillity which is not disturb'd by the Inequality of Condition'.[2]

At the time of Cook's arrival it is thought there were something like five hundred tribes of Aborigines, numbering maybe 300,000 people in all.

The decisive encounter between those who believed they stood for white Christian civilization and those whom they saw as the representatives of an unregenerate barbarism had happened. It was, I believe, very hard for the white men who first set eyes on Aborigines to see them with any clarity at all. So fixed were their own religious beliefs (in a way that divided humankind into Christians and infidels), so black and strange and naked did the Aborigines appear (and in white Europe black was the colour associated with the Devil), so little was the simplicity of the natural life admired by members of a civilization proud of its elaborate clothes, its huge buildings and complex crafts and artefacts, that the relative poverty, nakedness, blackness of the Aborigines immediately proclaimed them inferior and unregenerate. Artists' impressions of Aborigines drawn to celebrate both Captain

Cook's arrival and the arrival of the First Fleet eight years later show a gross exaggeration of the 'savagery' of the black population and bear little likeness to anything human at all. Indeed, what the artists unwittingly reveal is the general white belief that these people were 'not quite human'. It would be many years, and much blood would have flowed, before this damaging belief would be shifted and the wonderful gifts of the Aboriginal peoples – their courage, ingenuity, resourcefulness, aesthetic awareness and profound religious sense – would be recognized and acknowledged by white people.

There is a watercolour painting by Lieutenant William Bradley of the *Sirius*, part of the First Fleet, which shows 'The First Interview with Natives at Port Jackson in New South Wales'. Bradley had kept a journal which he illustrated himself of the British Fleet setting off from London with a cargo of convicts and arriving in what is now Sydney Harbour in 1778. The natives, very black and naked and numerous as ants, are ranged along the seashore with one or two clumsy boats, in contrast to the elegant sailing ship with its smart, blue-clad figures.

The First Fleet had made this long, difficult journey in keeping with Government policy. Because of the terrible poverty and criminality of its major cities, England's prisons were bursting to overflowing, and governments were unwilling to incur the cost of building new ones. England had already experimented with transportation to the plantations: convicts continued to be banished to the New World until, eventually, the American colonies rebelled and that particular way of getting rid of criminals was stopped. The crisis in housing British criminals grew and the Thames and the southern ports of England became crammed with the prison hulks which figure so horribly in Dickens's *Great Expectations*. Typhus, says Robert Hughes in *The Fatal Shore*, became endemic on the hulks, which caused panic that it would spread to the rest of the population.

By exporting its criminals eight thousand miles from home, into what appeared to be an empty country, England set about washing its hands of a threatening and intractable problem. It was comfortably suggested by politicians and others that, once the convicts had served their penal term and been reformed by it, they could set themselves up in farming or in other work and begin their lives anew.

It was a disastrous theory, little more than an excuse for 'dumping' huge numbers of citizens far enough away for it to be difficult for them ever to return. Transportation was punishment sometimes for major criminals and sometimes, particularly in the early years, for those guilty of little more than prostitution or stealing to relieve their hunger. After the nightmare eight-month-long voyage they had little to look forward to but life in a community of violence and despair. The penal colonies were famous for their brutality and cruel floggings; some were little more than concentration camps.

Remarkably, some of the convicts did rise above their circumstances. Such was the shortage of labour in the new colony that some of those who could read and write found jobs and later rose to senior positions. Some ex-convicts did go on to become farmers. Most were forbidden to return to Britain on pain of the death penalty.

It could not have been other than a rough society. It was, for many years, almost entirely male – women transported were liable to be prostitutes, thieves or murderers, and they were in a minority. Yet, impressively, when you think of their miserable beginning, freed criminals went on to set up the rudiments of stable societies and, gradually, to build a country – to the settlers in Australia it felt more like a group of different countries – to which emigrants in search of work, adventure and new opportunities soon came as readily as to America. The chronic poverty of nineteenth-century Britain drove wave after wave of Scots, Welsh, Irish and English away from peat bog, mountain, village and slum in an interminable exodus from a native land they could rarely hope to see again.

The story of the colonization of Australia is moving and terrible, an extraordinary account of human suffering, endurance and creativity, and of the odd kinds of hope and redemption humans find, or fail to find, for themselves in the grimmest circumstances. But it is only in very recent years that the heavy cost of Britain's eighteenth-century criminal policy has begun to emerge.

The European/white Australian view of the invasion was that it happened in a country that was empty. This fantasy, which came to prominence in the 'Mabo Case' – an important legal decision about land rights in 1992 – was that when the First Fleet arrived the country was *terra nullius*, an empty country, and thus, nobody's property, land to which no one had any claim. Of course, it had been known since Captain Cook's landfall in Australia that there were 'natives' there. But they were not particularly numerous, or unusually aggressive and, in the reckoning of House of Commons' committees and statesmen, their property rights were non-existent. They did not count as recognizable citizens.

As it happened, Aborigines never seemed to think of 'owning' land but rather of serving it, of living on it and off it and with it, by 'singing it', conducting ceremonies and rituals on it, by telling stories about it and about the Ancestors who shaped it. Certain parts of the country were particularly important to particular clans because particular stories were told about events that had occurred there. To this extent that landscape was more 'theirs' than it was somebody else's, and this sort of ownership would be respected by other clans.

This subtle grasp of reality was mostly lost upon the white invaders who simply saw black natives, for whom there were various insulting names, such as abo, boong, coon, (gin and lubra in the case of women). They were often assumed to be hostile and, equally, assumed to be genetically and humanly inferior, savages to be put down by brave white men as courageously as, in the old Hollywood movies, the Red Indians were quelled by the US Cavalry. Like the Red Indians or, as people say now, the native Americans, the Australian Aborigines were people with a long-standing workable way of life, an evolved spiritual sense and a profound wisdom to which the newcomers were entirely blind.

The clashes whenever and wherever they came were desperate, though they took many different forms. On 26 January 1788, eight months after they had set out from England, Captain Arthur Phillip and the eleven ships of the First Fleet arrived in Port Jackson (now Sydney Harbour) with 1030 people, 548 male and 188 female convicts. Phillip came with instructions from Britain to be on good and friendly terms with local populations. He favoured courteous meetings with local Aboriginal groups, coupled with gifts to gain their favour. In the words of the Australian historian Mary Durack,

> The people of the dream watched the people of the clock come out of the sea and strike their flagstaff firmly into the sand. They assumed that these pale-skinned mariners were the spirits of their ancestors returned from the islands of the dead and that they would act in accordance with ancient intertribal etiquette. When gifts were exchanged on the beach the only curious sign had been the eagerness of the newcomers to retrieve the ticking timepieces that the natives had found a diverting novelty, but this breach was forgiven as being an understandable lapse of memory.
>
> The strangers, for their part, secure in the certain values of expanding empire, had no doubt that the simple but apparently intelligent primitives would soon appreciate the blessings of civilization and gladly abandon their godless and feckless ways for those of a superior culture.
>
> Both people were mistaken, for the clock was not a toy but a way of life, as the Dreaming was a way of life, the one defining time by an arrow, the other in terms of heavenly bodies and seasonal change. Neither could appreciate the other's logic, but whereas the Aborigines learned to anticipate the white man's conduct with reasonable accuracy, they themselves were seldom, if ever, to behave as was expected.'[3]

The Aboriginals who lived in the area which came to be called Sydney were themselves a kind of aristocrat; Aboriginals so fortunate in their circumstances that life was easy for them and they had time to sit and enjoy the pleasures of existence. Fish and seafood of all kinds were plentiful in Sydney cove and the Paramatta river, the bush was full of game and it took a minimal amount of hunting in the easiest of conditions to feed well on possum and bandicoot and kangaroo, and to have fine fur to wear over one's shoulders in the cooler weather.

By the first winter after the arrival of the First Fleet all this was changed. With 150 convicts remaining, after others had been dispersed to other colonies, together with a large contingent of sailors, soldiers and officers, local fish supplies were already being depleted. Water was becoming polluted and the kangaroo population was hugely reduced.

The Aboriginal population became increasingly angry. They made raids on the camps of the invaders, stealing cattle and other food, which brought reprisals upon them, and worsened relations still further. Many of the white people whom they met were convicts working out in the bush, hardened recidivists who had led desperate lives. Brutalized and uneducated as they were, they had even less sympathy for and understanding of the Aborigines than the army officers who controlled them.

The crisis over the depleted food supplies was followed by the arrival of smallpox, hitherto unknown in Australia. The infection was, of course, introduced by the First Fleet, though they attempted to deny it when it became known back in England. The Aborigines had no resistance to it, and there are heartrending descriptions of little groups of them to be found out in the bush dying of the dreadful disease. It is estimated that by 1789 half the Aborigines in the Sydney basin had died of smallpox. Alcoholism and syphilis were two other scourges brought by the white man that would destroy more Aborigines. Denied female companionship, both soldiers and convicts had sexual relations with Aboriginal women. The Aboriginal Eden had been irrevocably destroyed.

Racked by these devastating events the Aborigines attempted a programme of resistance. A warrior called Pemulway assembled a fighting force of a hundred men to launch attacks on the invaders. Spears against guns made for hopeless odds, of course, and the brave Pemulway was killed.

The outcome was inevitable from the start. Resistance would always be overcome by British firepower and trained soldiery. Sometimes it was a quite gentle process, with intelligent officers who worked thoughtfully and sympathetically. More often it was a matter of brutality, the Aborigines shot down like animals. As the whites gradually began to inhabit other parts of Australia, setting up sheep stations, mining – for gold, opals, precious stones – as they began to build towns with schools, hospitals, shops, entertainments, so the fear of the black presence grew, much as the fear of the Indian grew in America.

Settlers saw the Aborigine as semi-human, a kind of mockery of their own civilized humanity and a threat to their own precarious, frugal lives, waiting to steal or kill. When they did get to know Aborigines, they had an uneasy sense of something almost uncanny about them, well-described by David Malouf in his novel *Remembering Babylon*. 'It brought you slap up against a terror you thought you had learned, years back, to treat as childish: The Bogey, the Coal Man, Absolute Night. And now here it is, not two yards away, solid and breathing . . .'[4]

Upon them they projected their fears of the unknown.

While some whites reacted only with fear of the Aborigines, others were influenced by some sense of the dignity of the 'noble savage'. Rousseau's idea of the grace of the natural man appealed to intellectuals among the colonizers. Captain James Stirling, a Scottish naval officer started the Swan River settlement in 1829, at what is now Perth, with a small company of soldiers and a group of Britons of good family together with their servants and labourers. There were two thousand people altogether, who had come out in fifty ships. Conditions were harsh for them. By 1830, there were no more than twenty houses, the country was less good for agriculture than they had hoped, and the grass not good for sheep. They were welcomed by local Aborigines and, in turn, Stirling placed them under the protection of the British Empire. But, as on the east coast, the white incomers began to deprive the Aborigines of hunting and fishing grounds, many of them of sacred importance; farmers simply annexed land and domesticated it, and the Aborigines themselves were driven away from the coast and into the less fertile mountains.

Within thirty years, the Swan River Aboriginal peoples were dying out, of hunger and sicknesses the white man had introduced. The white man moved inland with large flocks of sheep and encountered more aggressive Aborigines, though in places compromises were reached and Aborigines took work caring for stock, at which they were very able.

There had been convicts and soldiers, followed by those trying to make, or improve, their fortunes, and then there were the missionaries. Most of them, whether Catholic or Protestant, had an absolute conviction that the Aborigines needed the blessing of Christianity conferred upon them and a partial, or total, blindness to the profoundly spiritual nature of Aboriginal beliefs. They came to teach, not to listen. They were concerned about the physical welfare of Aborigines: they did not beat or overwork them as the sheepfarmers and station owners were to do; they often offered food and water, which made them an attractive port of call in times of hunger and drought; on many occasions they were to speak up as witnesses to acts of brutality or to murder of Aborigines. They were often good and loving people, yet their activities may have been as destructive of Aboriginal life as anything done by the soldiers, since they had a will to convert that was, in some cases, little more than a will to power.

The anthropologist, Catherine Berndt, made a faintly comic observation while doing fieldwork in the 1940s near a mission at Ooldea on the edge of the Great Victoria Desert in South Australia. Aboriginal hunting and gathering groups frequently 'came in' to the station at Ooldea, encountering white people for the first time. The most urgent concern of the missionaries was to cover their nakedness with clothing. At the first sign of smoke out over 'spinifex country,' which indicated the cooking fires of approaching Aborigines, the missionaries would start getting out clothes. It says something perhaps of the priority of prudery.

Other activities of the missionaries were more damaging. They made the nineteenth-century link between order and godliness, gathering

51

children into schools where they slept in dormitories, away from the influence of their parents, and imposing meticulous timetables upon them. The people of the clock were doing their best to impose their own obsession upon the people of the dream.

Worse followed. Like every culture, the Aborigines had spiritual leaders, those who had visions, dreams, insights, who guided a group or a clan in times of decision or uncertainty. Called variously *maparn, karadji, wingirin, kuldukke (maparnpa* in Kukatja, or *minyira* in the case of a woman) which may be translated as clever man, medicine man, healer, native doctor, sorcerer, shaman, or witch doctor, they were not necessarily sinister (though because of their power, all could be sinister if the need arose), but saw deeply into the meaning of things and had healing power in one form or another. When Aboriginal culture clashed with European culture and, in particular, when the power of the clever man clashed with the power of the Christian missionary, his wisdom (it was more often a man than a woman) was made a particular target of ridicule and obloquy. 'His importance as the guardian of traditional culture and sacred lore was progressively eroded [in the nineteenth and early twentieth century] to the point where he was regarded as no more than an imposter and tribal scamp.'[5] The medicine of the mission, dramatic in achieving certain sorts of pain relief or cures, made it seem that the religious power of the missionaries was superior to the power of the clever man or woman. But by discrediting such leaders the missions also damaged the powerful sense of group identity and meaning associated with religious ritual. The rituals themselves sometimes fell into disuse. This coincided with many changes which degraded Aborigines. Abandoning their traditional lives as warrior hunters to become employees of the white folk, Aborigines were seen as criminals and treated accordingly: chain gangs of Aborigines were a regular sight in parts of Australia until the early twentieth century. They began to suffer from imprisonment, alcoholism, urban poverty. Of course, the missionaries, in many ways caring deeply for the Aborigines, though often with arrogant ideas of conversion, had little idea of their own destructive powers.

Many of them lived and died heroically, striving to build missions in torturing climates, suffering from mosquitoes and fever and flies, often with a bitter sense of being forgotten by those at home. Mary Durack tells the story of Matthew Gibney, an Irish Catholic priest who was, in many ways, a good friend of the Aborigines. He arrived in Western Australia in 1863. Appalled at the treatment of Aboriginal prisoners – at the beating and chaining and, in particular, at the suffering of Aborigines working as divers on the pearling boats on the west coast – he dedicated his life to trying to help them. Once consecrated bishop, he encouraged the Trappist interest in Aboriginal conversion and welfare and helped set up a Trappist foundation near Beagle Bay. Bishop Gibney found the Aborigines 'a splendid race of men', as well as 'lovable' and 'docile'.[6]

The Trappists, however, despite the heroic asceticism for which they are famous, found the mission intensely difficult. Their garden was destroyed by cyclones and kangaroos, their health was destroyed by mysterious complaints, and the Aborigines, though friendly and ready to wear clothes, sing hymns and even learn Latin, seemed never to respond to the Christian message with the enthusiasm of African natives. Instead, they went through the motions and then disappeared to the bush to practise their own chanting, dancing and swinging of bullroarers, and where, there was reason to believe, the boys were undergoing initiation rites. The Trappists became convinced that babies were, from time to time, sacrificed to make special feasts for visiting tribesmen and this, whether a fantasy or not, upset them more than anything. Later, the monks were supplanted at the mission by the St John of God Sisters, who found the job almost equally disheartening.

The Australian continent evoked other kinds of heroism. The European invasion meant at first that there were citadels of British culture – at Sydney, South Australia, the Swan River and the North-West – and vast uncharted spaces inland. South Australia, founded in 1836, was the most successful of them in the early stages and rapidly became wealthy. Cereals and copper were the basis of their prosperity, but the wheatfields soon began to suffer from overuse, and it was decided to run large quantities of sheep. The settlers thought that if they explored the interior they might find new grazing lands, but every attempt to do so merely found formidable deserts to the north and north-east of Adelaide.

Western Australia, half a million square miles of unknown country, was 'the greatest absolute blank on the face of the globe apart from the Poles' as the Royal Geographical Society put it in 1868. This measured one fifth of Australia, and included the Gibson Desert, the Great Sandy Desert, and part of the Great Victoria Desert. Explorers had two ambitions, apart from the desire to find grazing land. One was to find the reputed 'inland sea', which would give an alternative source of water (it was assumed it would be fresh water). The other was to find a successful overland route between Adelaide and the Swan River Colony (the journey had always to be made by sea), preferably with grazing, so that animals could be driven from one to the other.

A number of explorers went in search of the inland sea and suffered appallingly on their travels, tortured by scurvy, insects, and heat so intense that it made their stirrup irons unbearably hot and the lead fall out of their shrinking pencils. They cheered themselves with the thought that they were bringing liberty, civilization and Christianity to 'the natives'. Union Jacks were planted on mountains and toasts raised to Queen Victoria on her birthday. Occasionally, they came across the Aboriginal peoples in their travels, and wondered at their ability to find water in places where white men were dying of thirst.

In 1855, Augustus Gregory approached the Great Sandy Desert – Kukatja country – from the north, sailing down the Victoria River. From Sturt Creek, near to Balgo, he commented on the 'red glare' of the sand, the salt lakes and the low rocky hills. He climbed Mt Wilson, noticing the sandstone hills in horizontal strata and the unbounded waste of sandy ridges that stretched before him. He travelled no further south.

Another explorer of the Great Sandy Desert was Colonel Peter Egerton Warburton, who set out from Alice Springs in April 1873, taking an Aborigine boy, Charley, along with his team.[7] In addition, there were two Arabs to manage seventeen camels. Studying earlier expeditions, Warburton had noted the severe problems spinifex grass posed for the horses. Its sharp spines scratched their legs, and the wounds quickly became infected and drew clouds of flies. Inevitably, the other problem on expeditions with a number of men and horses was the desperate shortage of water. It seemed to Warburton that camels might be a partial solution.

Despite the camels and a six-month-supply of food, the horrors of the expedition were many. By the twentieth day, they were already seriously short of water. On 1 May they crossed the Tropic of Capricorn at Haast Bluff, and shot some black cockatoos for food.

On 7 May they found themselves in dramatic countryside near Mt Wedge, where the 'stupendous rocks' terrified the camels. They found springs and running water – an enormous relief – and they continued 'westing' in good heart. On 22 May, disaster struck. They reached Eva Springs but, terrified at the sight of snakes, many of the camels bolted.

On 8 June, they entered Western Australia. A week later came the first real contact with Aborigines. It is not difficult to imagine the astonishment of a group of Aborigines, deep in their own tribal country, who had never seen a white man or a camel before in their lives. 'Surprised three blacks who fled from their camp at our approach,' Warburton writes in his journal. 'They left their fire burning and their weapons behind them. We took a boomerang for Charley, and left a piece of blanket in exchange.'[8] The 'decency' of this first encounter was not, unfortunately, typical of their later meetings with Aborigines.

Four days later they saw a *lubra* accompanied by a small boy and a baby. Their response was to chase her. Not surprisingly, the woman was terrified and, tossing away everything she was carrying except her baby, she escaped. The small boy was captured by Charley, however, and 'showed not the slightest fear' (perhaps he simply hid his feelings), 'but looked at us and our camels as if quite accustomed to the sight. We put him on the camel, in front of Charley, and made signs for him to show us where we could find water . . . He kept chattering and pointing to the west. We turned in that direction, but before we had got far, Charley's sharp eyes detected some diamond-sparrows rising from the ground. We had found a native well with some water. Offered the lad food and let him go.'[9]

In a lordly manner, Warburton ponders on the skill of Aborigines. 'It is curious to speculate on the instinct that enables the degraded inhabitants of this wilderness to find the few spots where the precious element is attainable. The savage has the advantage of the European in this respect. Out of forty-nine or fifty attempts made by the party to find water by sinking, only one was successful, although we brought all our experience and desertcraft to bear.'[10]

Like his predecessors, Warburton was learning another lesson about the ignorance of the European in 'the wilderness' as scurvy struck them. Hidden in a hole on top of a hill they found, as already mentioned, two *tjuringa* or sacred boards and noted the 'unintelligible scrawls' on them before throwing them away. The irony is that these scrawls, like most sacred boards, almost certainly gave information about the whereabouts of water.

By 10 July, one of the Arabs was so seriously ill with scurvy that he was given citric acid and a small yellow berry from the scrub recommended by Charley to cure him.

> Six natives came to the camp but we could not understand each other. We watched these scamps with the utmost care and closeness, as we thought, but they were too much for us, and stole an axe; this, of course, put an end to their visits . . . They were fine, well-made men, most of them bearded, and considering the wretched hand-to-mouth life they lead, were in very fair bodily condition. Clothing they possessed none; they were armed with spears and waddies or short clubs, the latter of which they use to knock over wallabies, a small species of kangaroo, on which they seem mainly to subsist.[11]

The party then found their way from Ethel Creek and Emily Springs to Bishop's Dell and, finally, Mt Wilson in Kukatja country. The view from Mt Wilson did not encourage Colonel Warburton. 'As the whole country was one vast desert, destitute of any indications of the existence of water, it was clear that no useful results could arise from an attempt to penetrate the inhospitable region.'

Then followed a rather degrading incident.

> Captured a young native woman; this was considered a great triumph of art, as the blacks all avoided us as though we had been plague-stricken. We kept her a loose prisoner, intending

that she should point out native wells to us; but whilst we camped today the creature escaped from us by gnawing through a thick hair-rope, by which she was fastened to a tree. We were quickly on her tracks, but she was too much for us, and got clear away. We had not allowed her to starve during her captivity, but she supplied herself from the head of a juvenile relation with an article of diet which our stores did not furnish.[12]

Behind his armour of European superiority, Warburton seems pitifully lacking in imagination, and the compassion that might flow from it. He cannot understand the Aborigines' sound instinct to keep well away from a party whose only intention is to exploit them, nor the kind of simplicity and poverty which might make even head lice a form of food. Yet he and his party cannot survive in the wilderness without a vast baggage of food and drink. Like many who were to follow him, he hardened his heart to Aboriginal suffering by pretending that 'these people' were not quite human, were little more than animals. The graces of an English gentleman fell quickly away from him, however:

Found a native camp and a well. Could not catch a native there, they being too quick for us; apart from, however, the camp a bawling, hideous old hag was captured, and we secured this old witch by tying her thumbs behind her back and haltering her by the neck to a tree. She kept up a frightful howling all night.[13]

When the prisoner could not, or would not, lead them to water, they let her go.

They found themselves on 'high table land', perhaps the cliff plateau of Balgo, and shot ducks, parrots and pigeons, but lacked satisfying food. They were tormented by ants, which ran over them and everything else, making it almost impossible to sleep or rest. (They did not know the Aboriginal trick of surrounding oneself, or the camp, with a ring of ashes.)

They continued 'westing', and trying to catch 'natives', who by now they called 'blackbirds'. They were driven, by severe hunger, to eat their camels, eating some of the meat cooked fresh and 'jerking' the rest to chew on their travels. So bitter was their need that they learned by painful necessity how to make even the feet edible, cutting them off at the hock, and singeing them over embers. Then the whole foot was placed on the embers until the sole was so charred it came off with a blow. After that, it was necessary to put the foot in a bucket and boil it vigorously for thirty-six hours. 'Then at last you may venture to hope that your teeth – if good – will enable you to masticate your long-deferred dinner.'[14]

Inevitably, there was a confrontation with the Aborigines. Warburton was out looking for water when 'hearing a light noise behind me, I turned and beheld nine armed blacks running towards me. We stopped and faced each other about fifteen yards apart; two youngsters poised their spears at me, but I think it was more out of bravado than anything else. For when I advanced upon them, pistol in hand, they lowered their spears.'[13] Eventually, Warburton achieved a sort of working friendship with this band of warriors and bartered with them for a wallaby. His published account of his journey was illustrated with a kind of *Boys' Own Paper* lithograph of the brave officer standing alone against a bunch of horrid savages.

Warburton was learning a little from Aboriginal example. In his desperate need he discovered that snake was tasty. 'A snake nicely roasted in the ashes is a delicacy not despised by bushmen who have good beef and mutton at their command, and is a favourite article of diet with the natives throughout the Australian continent.'[14] Perhaps it was from his Aboriginal contacts he learned to roast and eat acacia seeds. They could not help him with the persistent flies which, if there was the slightest abrasion of the skin, caused festering and, eventually, a nasty wound. The men spread Holloway's ointment round their eyes but could do little else to protect themselves.

Eventually, having traversed the Great Sandy Desert from east to west, Warburton reached Roebourne on the coast, after a terrible 4000-mile journey. Only two of the seventeen camels remained. He travelled to Fremantle, Perth and Albany by ship and was feted at each before sailing for England, where he would give his lecture to the Royal Geographical Society.

CHAPTER FIVE

In my room was an introduction to Balgo on writing paper headed, The Northern Jesuit Community, and it said that I, like all other guests, was invited to join the Jesuits for breakfast 'at any time after 6.30 a.m.'. So next day I showed up for cornflakes, toast and instant coffee in the kitchen. There, I met Fr. Brian, a compact, wiry figure in his forties, with a wry expression that I liked at once. He had only arrived at Balgo a few months before, as the Jesuits had only recently been invited to join the Wirramanu community, but he had had twenty years of working with Aborigines, most of that at Port Keats, and he had also been a researcher for the Royal Commission into Black Deaths in Custody. By chance he had once worked as a student at Balgo, so that now he was strengthening links with adult Aborigines he had first known when they were children. There was touching evidence of this in a book of photographs of Balgo and its people taken in his student days. It sat on the kitchen table and was much pored over by visitors.

'Look, there's my brother! That's my Dad!'

'So what's the Catholic Church doing here?' I could not resist asking.

'I'm always asking myself that,' Brian answered. I felt, as I was later to feel quite often, how honest and thoughtful he was about the Catholic presence at Balgo, how he never took it for granted.

Not then, but a few days later, I told him about my sense of shyness with Aborigines.

'That's right,' he said unexpectedly. 'You should be shy. It's the people who don't have any doubts that I mistrust. Tell people something about yourself – tell them that you are married, and about your children. That's the great link.'

Later we talked about the importance of introducing me to the chairman of the Aboriginal Council, John Lee.

'But we can't use his name at the moment.'

'How do you mean?'

'It's *kumentjayi*.'

'Sorry?'

'It means that it is the name of someone who has just died and no one is allowed to use the name for a long time afterwards. We would say "This is Kumentjayi Lee." John is out of bounds for now, along with quite a lot of other names.'

'Isn't that very difficult?'

'Fairly. You get used to it.'

'So when can you start using it again?'

'That's the difficult one. The rule-of-thumb is to do it when you hear people doing it. The Aborigines have some unspoken way of working out when the time has come and I just take my cue from them.'

I was to find that this *tabu* extended not only to living people. The name of John the Baptist came up in one of the Easter services and was adapted by the speaker to 'Kumentjayi Baptist'. Other names, I discovered, that were currently *kumentjayi* were Peter, David, Stephen, Paul, Francis, Frank, James, Joe, Richard, Gary, Charles, Joseph, Christopher, Mary, Veronica, Theresa, Irene, Jane, Kerry and Topsy.

My first day happened to be Maundy Thursday, and I knew that the Easter services began that evening.

'What time is the service?'

Brian grinned.

'When it happens. When enough people turn up.'

'But how will I know?'

'Oh, you'll know. When you hear the bell ring, then come on over to the church about half an hour after that, then we may be beginning. Or we may not. If you are seeing the Sisters this morning would you ask them if we could borrow their fairylights? It's too hot to hold the service in the church, so we thought we'd have it outside on the grass and rig up the lights along the outside of the church.'

Already I was beginning to discover something of the leisureliness of Balgo. Time seemed unimportant – things happened when they happened or not at all – and the middle part of the day was swallowed by sleep and lethargy, since between about eleven and four the heat and glare made it difficult to spend long outside. As in all hot countries any action took place in the early morning and in the late afternoon and evening. I thanked my lucky stars for the fan and airconditioner in my room which made the heat of the day bearable.

In the late afternoon I went for a walk.

'What happens if you get lost in the desert?' I had asked one of the Sisters the night before. I had once, in Sinai, had this alarming experience, walking in a pleasant daze, forgetting to notice landmarks. There had been a frightening couple of hours while I anxiously calculated how little water I had left.

'You take matches,' one of them said, 'and you use some of the dry vegetation to make a fire. By day people can see the column of smoke miles away, and by night they can see the light of the fire.' I decided to keep some matches in my trouser pocket, though I soon discovered that on foot, at least (it was different by car), it was quite difficult to get lost at Balgo. I also took a stick with me, fearful of some Australian snake I had heard about – a king snake, was it? – that came straight for you if it saw you. I wasn't sure if that kind of snake inhabited this desert and I thought people might laugh at me if I asked.

Within about ten minutes of leaving the centre of Balgo I found myself in a very beautiful place. There was a canyon – two tall red mesa facing one another across a small ravine. It felt like being in a countryside of two storeys. I did not attempt the summits of the canyon, but instead took the path down between them, a passage of brilliant red that led out into an oceanic expanse of sand, small rocky mesa rising here and there on the horizon. One double mesa had an Aboriginal name that translated as 'Two Milks'. It was difficult to believe the tide would not shortly be creeping back over the endless sand ridges. It was aeons since the sea had withdrawn for the last time, yet I had never been in an inland place so like a seashore. High in the blue sky were long cigar-shaped clouds I had seen on the prairies of America, but never in England.

The plants were fascinating. There were endless pincushion-shaped mounds of spiny grass that give this part of Australia the name of 'spinifex desert'; there was a small creek with casuarina growing alongside it. By the side of the track were wattles, in beautiful mimosa-like flower, and mulga. (I remembered that in the Sinai desert acacia was the only tree that would grow and that the Children of Israel had therefore used it to fashion the Ark of the Covenant.) There was an exquisite pink flower, a little like a poppy, with a deep-red heart, which I later identified as Sturt's Desert Rose, yellow and lilac convolvulus, and the bright yellow-and-purple flower of the potato bush. The whole landscape had much more vegetation than usual, I knew, because the recent Wet had been so copious, germinating seeds that had been in the ground for years.

I heard a whistling bird, unseen, which sounded so much like a human being whistling a few melodic notes, that I kept looking for the whistler. Later, I heard the bird many times, and wondered whether it was the kingfisher or *luurnpa*, one of the totemic ancestors of the Kukatja, and after whose epic journey Wirrumanu was named.

Some weeks later I went back to that part of the desert with two of the younger Aboriginal women, Helen and Ruthie. Indicating the mesa and the deep holes in its side, Ruthie said, 'Kingfisher.'

'Now, or in the Dreamtime?' I asked, wanting to verify that king-fishers still lived there.

Ruthie looked at me as if this was an entirely meaningless question. 'Kingfishers,' she replied, with an expansive gesture.

Much later, back in Perth, I looked up kingfishers and decided the Balgo kind must be the White-tailed Kingfisher, which lives along the creeks of desert places.

We gathered for the first of the Easter services on the grass outside the church. The bell had gone, I had waited for half an hour as instructed and, when I could hear the occasional strumming of a guitar, I wandered out across the sand with my torch. It was a hot night, the stars were brilliant, and there was a full moon. I picked out the Southern Cross, wondering, as I always do in the southern hemisphere, at finding myself under a strange sky with only Orion, the hunter, lying on his side, reminding me of my native northern heaven. Only a few weeks before coming to Balgo, I had camped with friends on the shores of the Red Sea and had been unable to sleep for watching the progress of Orion as it slowly dipped behind the horizon. I remembered an Englishwoman I had once met in Australia, one of the '£10 Poms' who were encouraged to help populate Australia after the Second World War, who had told me how her feeling of acute homesickness had slightly eased whenever she saw Orion in the sky.

Brian had rigged up the line of fairylights along the eaves of the church which gave the occasion a holiday air, and a spotlight shone on the area below them, a sort of grassy stage. There was a small table covered in an uneven cloth, which held several chalices – it was a bit like a school prizegiving – and there was water in a carved tree trunk. Behind this modest altar were a few chairs for the priests, the chairman, Kumentjayi Lee, and one or two other people who had key roles to play in the service. On one side of this open-air chancel were a group of Aboriginal women who would form the choir, many of them accompanied by tiny naked children.

As the grassy space filled up I became aware of the dogs running amongst us, dogs that had a look of the bull terrier about them but also with a distinct dingo appearance – a squareness around the head. Dogs, I knew, had been vital in the hunting days but, nowadays, with much less hunting, every family seemed to have two or three. One or two of them were lame, and some seemed to have skin diseases. Soon I noticed that a bitch was being pursued by several dogs in and out among the worshippers and that, in the intervals of following her, the dogs fought angrily with each other. As the service began it was sometimes hard to hear the words above the noise of yapping dogs. The young children, in contrast, were quiet and content, making little excursions away from their mothers to look at other children or to greet grown-ups they recognized. On the far side of the altar was the band, or orchestra – some guitar players with their electrical equipment, and a didgeridoo player. The young men sat in a group behind them.

Leaning against the wall of the church were huge paintings which, though apparently abstract, I knew to be about the Passion of Jesus. 'We treat the Passion story as a sort of journey or Dreaming story of the last days of Jesus,' Brian had told me. 'That makes a lot of sense here.' I took this to mean that the story of Jesus, like the story of the animal Ancestors, was woven right through the fabric of living, was part of 'how things are'. Like the totem stories, like the stories that were danced and sung in annual Aboriginal ceremonies, the Jesus story needed 'investment' – it needed a regular space in which to be recalled and lived through and more thoroughly understood. This was an instance of the Dreaming, the bridge between eternity and time, between the Ancestors and our living selves.

The congregation went on arriving – I could see why there had been no hurry – and finding places on the grass or sitting on oil drums or soft-drink crates. The women, girls and older men sat well forward. Young men drove up in cars – mostly old bangers – some from just a few hundred yards away. They sat up on the bonnets watching from the back with an air of detachment that suggested they might take off at any moment. Unlike the rest of the gathering they, at least, were not entirely committed.

In the course of the afternoon people had driven in from the outstations – 'the Billiluna mob', 'the Mularn mob' and the 'Yagga Yagga mob'. Such journeys at this time of year were no joke. Between Balgo and Billiluna the road was still officially closed and flooded to a depth of several feet. Nevertheless, the Billiluna mob had arrived, and several sisters who worked at the outstations had driven over, bringing elderly or very young passengers. Balgo was finding a sort of unity for Easter. 'We are all one people,' went one of the hymns, blithely ignoring the fact that members of at least three other tribes apart from the Kukatja were present. 'She my sister, he my brother.'

I found a makeshift seat next to Sister Marie from Lake Gregory, a round and rosy sister, with a subversive sense of humour, with whom I felt an instant sense of rapport. I had something on my mind.

'I'm not a Catholic,' I felt obliged to say. 'I'm an Anglican. I wouldn't like to give offence by taking communion.'

She laughed in pure astonishment. 'You don't think we'd mind *here*?' she said and, of course, immediately the idea did sound rather silly.

At odd intervals that day I had been looking up Kukatja words and trying to pronounce them, though I had not really got beyond saying 'Uwey' – Yes – and 'Wia' – No. She, I knew, had only recently come to the desert and I wondered how she was doing.

'I asked what language they'd like me to learn at Mularn and they said Walmajarri, so I'm doing my best with that,' she said. 'I'm not good at it.'

A small girl of about three came and wriggled on to Sister Marie's lap. She had a pretty face, with brilliant black eyes, but her expression was spoiled by a rope of snot on her upper lip. She was racked at intervals by a bad cough.

Cheryl, alarmed by the recent death from mosquito virus, was going round spraying everyone with insect repellent.

The singing was deep and musically eclectic, with bits of Country and Western, touches of the popular religious music from the French Catholic community of Taizé, and other songs that sounded as if they came from deep wells of Aboriginal rhythm and melody. We sang sometimes in English, sometimes in Kukatja, sometimes in Walmajarri and sometimes in Jaru. Most of the congregation joined in with clapping sticks. Two big fires gave off a strong, smoky smell.

Rather like a pantomime in which the women sing and the men sing, and the people in the stalls, or the people in the circle, do their separate bit, the different language groups did their bit.

'Would the Mularn mob like to sing to us?' Brian would ask. 'The Yagga Yagga mob?'

Soon it was obvious the whole thing would go on for hours – it was not one of those hour-long Masses familiar to urban Catholics, but a process that people slowly worked or wound themselves into. We had not cared what time the service started and we did not care when it was going to end.

Instead of the gospel being read out from the Bible (somehow an incongruous practice with pre-literate people), women stood beside the altar in front of the huge paintings of the Passion and told the story indicated by the picture in three different local languages. 'Here is the supper of Jesus . . . here is Jesus walking to Calvary . . .' Obviously deeply moved by the pathos of it, they sounded near to tears. As with the Dreaming stories of kangaroo and rainbow snake and other creatures so, for the length of the ritual, they gave themselves up unreservedly to the Christian passion story.

'There is more identification with the crucifixion story than with the resurrection,' Sister Marie whispered to me. 'Perhaps because they have such a deep sense of suffering.' I have a feeling she was talking not simply of the suffering inflicted by the coming of the white man, but of the ancestral experience of pain and hardship – thirst, hunger, heat, disease, childbirth – of a people living in one of the harshest climates in the world. Certainly pain and the ability to bear it was a crucial part of initiation ceremonies for young men as they became adults.

We prayed to 'Mama kamkara', the father in heaven, and to 'Tjitju', Jesus. Then there was a washing of feet. Women seemed readier than men to volunteer for this but soon there was a group sitting by the altar having their feet washed, and Cheryl was persuaded to join them. Cheryl, a greatly loved nursing sister, was about to leave the Balgo community and this service was in the nature of a farewell to her. As it gradually grew darker the headlights of the cars were turned on, which made the liturgy feel like a scene in a theatre.

The small girl wriggled down from Marie's lap, leaving a large wet stain on her skirt and a red sandy one where she had leaned her head against her shoulder.

As Brian raised the chalice there was a full-scale dog fight going on at his feet, with people yelling and hitting at their dogs and the dogs themselves absorbed in battle.

Later, when the service was over I stood enjoying the stars and gazing up at the Southern Cross. 'Do you know the expression,' Cheryl asked me, '"when the Southern Cross turns over"? It's an old stockmen's expression. "Wake me when the Southern Cross turns over". In the small hours you see it from a quite different angle.'

As I walked home thinking about the Southern Cross a small boy passed me on a bicycle. 'Hiya, Sistah! What your nem?' I seemed to have acquired a protective identity.

I woke very early next morning and discovered the strange and beautiful light described in the Kukatja language as *rakarra-rakarra*, the dawn-dawn, the first hint of day that creates an extraordinary illusion that light comes from inside the polished white trunks of the ghost gums and the deep red of the earth beneath them. I got up and went out for a walk in the desert, this time along the top of one of the canyons. Once again it was like being at a seaside place, standing on the cliff this time and looking out over a boundless ocean with a few little rocky islands dotted in it, only, as in the Revelation of St John, there was 'no more sea'. I found myself noticing for the first time something that I would notice repeatedly in Balgo. Looking at the many different shades of red – the dark gingerbread colour of the mesa still in shadow, the rose-red of the cliff I stood upon, the yellowy-red of the distant desert, the near vermilion of the sand as the sun blazed upon it – I caught myself thinking 'Just like Devon!', remembering the Sidmouth cliffs or the deep red of ploughed Devon soil. Of course, it wasn't that much like Devon, but I was finding a need to interpret or translate the unfamiliar and the startling in terms of the familiar and the comfortable. Generations of homesick Europeans in the past had done something very similar. Australian art galleries are full of nineteenth-century paintings depicting the wildness of the Outback and its innumerable gum trees exactly like a gentle Surrey view or a stand of larch trees.

Standing on the cliff I could see what looked like a horse or mule in the distance, and remembered that as I walked the floor of the desert I had noticed hoof marks. There were prints on the sandy ground of the cliff, too, not of horses, but of places where a scaly tail, a muscular body or tiny feet had slid or pattered over the ground, or others where a scuffle had taken place, and some bigger creature had found its dinner. An Aboriginal hunter, I reflected, would know not merely what this beautiful natural calligraphy spelled out, but how recently the animal had passed that way, and whether it was slow enough to be worth pursuing. I compared my own inability to observe landmarks. I thought of the innumerable times that, withdrawn into my thoughts, I had lost my way in both city and country, 'coming to', as it were, and not knowing where I was. I began to see it as a sort of disrespect or lack of love for the world of matter, displaced by the world of the mind. It seemed to me that it was a spiritual failing. But my education, like that of all Westerners, had prized words, reading, ideas above everything; it trained me to live in an inner world. Sensation – smell, touch, taste, colour, the world of early childhood in my case, but that of all pre-literate people throughout their lives – took a back seat as the fascination of reading took hold, substituting thought for observation. There was no voice to point out that there was loss as well as gain, that some essential connection with matter and with the body was in danger of being lost. This was mirrored by the dominant religious belief of the West – Christianity – which in practice valued spirit above matter. (Not in theory, though, since the key Christian belief is about the Word becoming flesh in the person of Jesus.)

An Aboriginal child learns not only an exact sense of direction but perpetual and minute observation of its surroundings. For inhabitants of a desert, survival may depend upon such awareness. In the book *Jilji*, in which the Aboriginal painter, Jimmy Pike, describes to an author, Pat Lowe, the way everyday things are understood by the Walmajarri people in the Great Sandy Desert, there is an account of the way the points of the compass are part of common parlance and understanding.

> Left and right are terms not much used. The closest equivalents, applied to people . . . mean strong side and weak side, but they are never used to indicate direction or place. In contrast, the six directional names: east, west, north, south, up and down are in constant use, not only in references to travel but also in discussions of the relative positions of people and objects over even the smallest spaces and distances. One person might ask another to move a piece of

meat on the fire a fraction to the east, or to pick up a stick lying to the north of his foot. Having his back scratched, a man will direct his wife 'Down, down . . . up. Yes. Now north a bit −north. West . . . that's it!'[1]

One of the Sisters described playing Kim's Game with Aboriginal children − the memory game we used to play at parties in my childhood where a tray of objects was briefly shown to us, then withdrawn, and a prize went to the child who wrote down the largest number. Some children used to remember a good many objects, some barely any. Aboriginal children, said the nun, simply remember all of them. For them there's no element of competition in the game at all.

I heard the haunting, operatic whistling sound again, as if Mozart was trying out a few bars to himself, and I saw a large black and white bird in a tree not far away. Was this the *luurnpa*? It did not look like any kingfisher I had ever seen, but I thought if I got closer I might see whether it had that short-necked look, or the distinctive beak. Stumbling through the rough grass I gave it ample opportunity to notice my approach. It watched me cynically for a while (so it seemed to me), but as soon as I got near enough to take a proper look, it flew away. I had been out in the desert for nearly two hours and was hungry. Also the sun was now blazing, the flies were settling on my face and arms and soon, I knew, I would be longing for the shade. But I had discovered the joys of the desert in the very early morning, and it would be the first of many days that I got up before dawn, watched the mysterious inner light in the gum trees and the sand while I drank a cup of tea, and then wandered out into the desert, trying not to disturb any of the scary Aboriginal dogs in the process, 'cheeky' dogs as people called them. (The word 'cheeky' had a special connotation at Balgo, meaning anything from downright aggressive to highspirited or playful. Thus the fierce local dogs were cheeky, but so were the adolescent girls who liked to tease.)

69

By nine the heat was already beginning to paralyse and I was glad to escape to my room where the fan had been running all night and to switch on the airconditioner. I listened with awe when Brian described how, as a student priest at Balgo, he had lived there without air-conditioning.

'When the temperature got over body temperature [37.5°] then you felt as if the heat was pouring off the walls and on to you,' he said. I thought of the generations of missionaries and others who had braved the intolerable heat in thick habits and suits, starched headdresses, Victorian corsets, and marvelled at the human capacity to suffer voluntarily in pursuit of an ideal. I had less capacity for suffering and soon learned that between eleven and four it was better to avoid the fierce glare and reflected heat of the sand and to stay indoors, reading, writing, sleeping. It was the most restful existence I had had for years.

At Sister Cecilia's suggestion I visited the Adult Education Centre on the day after my arrival where a group were printing T-shirts to wear on a planned trip to Melbourne. They were yellow, with a design of boomerangs and snakes printed on them, and I was given one, which I still wear and treasure. Suddenly, the Chairman Kumentjayi Lee arrived, and the discussion about when and where to introduce me to him was ended. He was a huge man, with a mane of hair like a lion, and I shook hands avoiding prolonged eye contact in the way I had been taught. My impression was that he was not pleased at yet another white person showing up. 'Too many *kartiya*!' I knew he had recently growled to Brian.

Around four o'clock that first Friday – Good Friday – I went to the store and discovered that at Balgo the time between four and five was not unlike the *passegiata* in an Italian town, a time when people came out to see and be seen. There was a bandstand used for rock concerts where the teenage girls, nicely dressed in skirts and T-shirts, sat and preened themselves. There were shady places under the trees where mothers and small children, often accompanied by grandmothers, sat quietly. There were little boys riding rapidly about on bicycles, shouting to one another. There were young men standing in groups, teasing one another and keeping an eye on the girls. There were often several groups playing cards. I particularly enjoyed watching the old men. Skinny, but lithe in movement, they often moved with an unconscious elegance, which was sometimes borne out by their clothes. A huge straw hat, or a pair of white trousers, gave them a seigneurial air.

'Do you ever feel afraid of the Aborigine men?' I asked Brian.

'I did sometimes at first. And then when I got to know them I found they were full of kindness. What is harder is their sense of being somehow inferior to me. I don't know how to shift that.'

The young women were often slim and graceful but the old women, or indeed most women once they had had children, seemed to grow not so much fat as shapeless, perhaps because the diet, no longer traditional, was not good. But dressing in not-very-becoming skirts and T-shirts, they too could occasionally find a pleasing elegance. There were a number of hats around in the Aboriginal colours of black, red and orange. Perched on the dark hair of the older women they had a wonderfully daring and rakish look.

The store was a huge prefab with the feel of an aeroplane hangar. I could find no butter or fresh milk. There was cheap white bread, tinned vegetables, Weetabix, sardines, rice, baked beans, peanut butter, cocoa, Milo, powdered milk, tea, instant coffee, instant cake mix, jelly and a Kraft margarine, unpleasantly called 'Coon'. There was a section of vegetables and fruit. The freezer had many lumps of frozen meat, kangaroo tail, chops, steaks.

The store in the late afternoon was a centre of buzzing social life. I bought some of the tired vegetables and fruit – they had had a long journey from the parts of Australia where apples or onions or carrots might be grown – and some instant coffee and biscuits. Chocolate was guarded in a sort of iron cage and had to be specially asked for. I noticed a shelf with innumerable sprays and lotions to deal with insects: fly sprays, cockroach repellents, mosquito coils and remedies for lice and fleas. In general, the contents of the store were those of a corner shop on a housing estate, the fare of those whose diet reflects an endemic poverty and who have little choice but to live on bread, jam, baked beans, sweet cakes and other cheap and filling food.

As I paid, a painfully thin man with a tousled, grizzled head mumbled something to me that I did not catch. I turned to him and, without really speaking, he made it clear that he hoped I would buy him a can of Coke. Others averted their eyes. It was obvious that he was a little mad, and I bought the can and gave it to him. After that I ran into

Ned many times in different parts of the camp usually accompanied by a faithful dog, who would growl if I got too close. Often he tried to speak to me, and it always felt as if he was articulating some form of distress, but I could not understand.

On Good Friday evening there was another service, held against a wonderful pink and green sky which slowly darkened. There was a ritual of 'touching the Cross' – a long line of people waiting their turn to touch the crucifix in a loving way almost as if Christ himself still hung upon it – which was very moving. Then there was a 'smoking' ceremony for those, mostly babies, who would be baptized, according to the ancient Christian practice, at the Easter Mass. A number of green branches were lit near to the altar, until we could only see it dimly through the clouds of smoke. One by one the babies were carried through it, and the adults to be baptized walked through it alone. What did it mean? Some said that it drove away evil spirits, others that it made you strong, which perhaps are two ways of saying the same thing.

On Saturday morning Robin came to breakfast saying that he'd just had a telephone call telling him that one of the old women, Wintja, had died up in the camp.

'Any special instructions?' he asked Brian.

'Anoint,' said Brian. 'Try to reduce people's fear. Scatter some holy water around.'

Wintja was old and had suffered from senile dementia for some time. She had taken to wandering, and once had fallen over one of the canyons and suffered broken legs. The Sisters had resisted all attempts to take Wintja away and put her in an institution, feeling that the safety would be outweighed by the utter loneliness of the life. So everyone had done their best to keep an eye on her, including, so the apocryphal story went, a tame emu, which used to follow her and peck her when she wandered too far from camp.

When Robin arrived at her house that morning he found that Wintja was not dead at all but was lying quietly in bed surrounded by one or two friends. He anointed her and sat beside her, while her friend Charlie brushed the flies away, and she died an hour later. Now there was the job of contacting her family, not all of whom lived locally.

'One son lives on a dried-up river bed miles away. How do we get hold of him?'

I soon became aware of the way the Kukatja think of death. On the one hand, like all Aboriginal people, they are pragmatic about it. In the old days of nomadic living an old person who could not walk any longer, or a handicapped baby, might threaten the lives of a whole family. On the other hand, as Brian's response to Robin showed, there was much fear around death, chiefly fear that the spirit of the dead person might endanger the living, perhaps by envy.

The Saturday night Mass was the first of Easter and a big crowd was expected. There were rumours of painting up, ceremonial dancing, and the cooking and eating of meat, probably kangaroo. The service was much longer than the previous one and ended with Brian laying hands on anyone who wanted it. One or two of the very old, I could not help noticing, received Communion twice because everyone was so anxious to make sure they were not left out. I was moved by a very old man, actually a famous Aboriginal painter, now blind and very infirm, stumbling up to the altar, pointing to his eyes and ears and having them touched and blessed. At one point in the service, a dog and a bitch were having intercourse in the shadows just beyond the spotlight.

As the service ended, soft drinks were given out to the children. There was some sort of altercation going on in the Aboriginal community, and gradually everyone drifted away. No dancing, no feast.

'What happened to the ceremonial idea?' I asked later, disappointed.

'You never quite know how people come to decisions here, nor what will happen until it does happen. But unlike Westerners Aborigines don't do something if they don't feel in the mood for it.'

The whitefellas' feast took place later at the Sisters' house where we had traditional roast lamb and all the little extras. I had a slight sense of a group of expats having a reassuring celebration in a foreign land, except that I was the only person there who was actually a foreigner.

CHAPTER SIX

Finding myself in a world where so many ideas and customs were different, I was particularly curious about two things. One was the way children were cared for and brought up; the other was the relation between men and women.

In the old days, children had taken as much part as they were able in adult activities. When they were very tiny they would either be carried by their mother as she went out 'gathering', or left behind with the old people in the camp. As soon as they could walk, both boys and girls went out gathering with the women and, from the age of six or seven, boys began to be included in the men's hunting expeditions.

My impression at Balgo was that children were treated with great gentleness and understanding. I never saw a child struck, or heard one shouted at. A book compiled for the teachers at Luurnpa School, *The Teacher's Handbook* was full of warnings of the dangers of making children feel 'shame'. A teacher who found a child naughty or lazy was advised to speak at once to its parents.

All little children were surrounded with female love and attention. Often in the cool of the late afternoon the smallest children would be sitting out on a blanket with several female relatives – their granny, auntie and big sister, maybe, as well as mother. The care of the children was not simply the mother's task, but that of the extended family. In some cases, younger women had gone off and left their children to the care of their mothers. Little children always seemed to be being held, cuddled, included, and they seemed happy and confident, both with one another and with grown-ups. In older children there was a rather appealing cheekiness – I remember three naked little boys of about seven at a church service moving from pew to pew in fits of giggles while Robin tried vainly to make himself heard.

Women played the traditional female role, staying at home, caring for the children, cooking, 'being there' for their husbands. Now that gathering was no longer crucial to survival, as it had been in the lives of the older women at Balgo, they fell into the housewife role that most women fulfilled in my youth in England, and that many women in Europe still live even today. A few worked as assistants at the school or the Adult Education Centre. A number of the older ones made money as artists – painting the abstracts for which Balgo has become well known.

The younger women, it seemed to me, were dependent, both emotionally and economically, on their menfolk and this made them vulnerable in the way it has always made women. There was some battering, particularly when the men got hold of 'grog'; there was relief sometimes when a violent man was away in prison; there was distress when a loved husband left Balgo to chase another woman. Soon after I left Balgo a woman was killed by an angry and drunken husband.

It seems to me, though, that I only knew about the violence by hearsay. What was much more obvious was that, a lot of the time, men and women led very separate lives, finding a lot of their happiness and most of their social life with members of their own gender. The older women, a number of whom were either widowed or had been left by their husbands, seemed to have a different kind of confidence and independence. The faces were lined by hardship and by years in the baking sun, but the impression was not of the frailty of age, but rather of something strong, formidable, indestructible.

An opportunity to spend time alone with the women arose when I was taken out on a gathering expedition by them – in this case to collect *tjunda* or bush onions. (Because of the store, gathering was no longer an essential routine, but the women still liked to do it fairly regularly, as the men still liked to hunt.)

With me squashed in the driving seat next to one of the older women and a dozen women and children in the back, Robin drove us for an hour or so out into the desert to the place they suggested, a one-storey house, covered in creeper, that Jimmy Moldavi, a former

Balgo resident, had built for himself. It was a very windy day, but that did not seem to reduce the intense heat.

Bush vegetables ripen in a procession through the course of the year: bush onions, bush tomatoes, bush potatoes, bush bananas, bush plums. On every outing, I noticed how women kept a sharp eye on the local vegetation, commenting on how plants were coming along and when they would be ready for harvesting. The look of the plants did not seem to bear much resemblance to the vegetable names used to describe them – they must have been invented to explain their edibility to the *kartiya*.

We stopped in a sort of field with sand dunes to one side, a field that was covered with a light veil of grasses. Unerringly, the women went to the bush onion grass and started digging with sticks or with flat stones. The children, all quite small, squatted down beside them and worked very hard, often using their hands. The onions were quite deep and it took energetic digging to get them out. They were white and tiny, about the size of a spring onion, and the big jam tins the women had brought with them filled only slowly. Tutored by them, I tried to find a similar patch of grasses, and thought that I had, but strenuous digging produced no onions at all.

As bare feet walked backwards and forwards across the sand, I was fascinated by the clarity of the footprints and realized how precisely these were reproduced in Aboriginal art. In paintings they usually indicated a journey.

By midday it was desperately hot. I tried escaping the sun by sitting in the truck, but it was very hot in there, too, and the flies tortured me. When they had got enough onions, the women lit a fire and baked the onions in the ashes. Sitting beside it alongside them – I was so hot by now that the heat of the fire seemed to make little difference – I tried to learn the correct pronunciation.

'*Tjunda.*'

'*Tjunda.*'

'*Tjunda.*' The women were polite and patient in repeating the word, as they always were when I tried to use a little Kukatja vocabulary, but it was clear that my pronunciation was not right. They gave me some baked *tjunda* anyway. They had a flavour a bit like sweet potato, pleasant, but not in the least like onion.

It took them several hours to find enough onions to feed perhaps twenty people. By then they had decided they had had enough onions and would go hunting sand frogs instead. It gave a fascinating insight into the sheer labour of the hunting-gathering life in the desert.

Traditional food-searching was shaped by the peculiar opportunities and demands of a semi-nomadic life and, in harsh dry climates, like that of Kukatja country, people tended to be more nomadic than in the lusher country of, say, eastern Australia. Meggitt describes how, among the Warlbiri, as late as 1960, food largely prescribed the social, and even the ceremonial, life.

The big ceremonies, in which large groups congregated, had to take place in the 'good season', which usually lasted from autumn until early winter, when billabongs were full and vegetable food plentiful.

Fairly large groups travelled from one waterhole to another as particular plants ripened and the game moved ahead of the hunters. As water and food became more scarce, the main party broke up into smaller groups. By the end of the dry weather, in late spring and early summer, the typical food-gathering unit comprised a man, his wives and children with, perhaps, an old widowed mother or father-in-law in their care. Only a group as small as this could find enough food to feed itself and their diet for a day might consist of a lizard or two, a few withered yams and a handful of grass seeds. As the rains broke and food gradually became plentiful again, so the small groups gradually converged until they became a large group once more.

Like the Warlbiri, the Kukatja and the Walmajarri divided themselves for living and hunting purposes into small family groups, moving in a wide sweep across 'Kukatja country' and 'Walmajarri country', before joining up again with the larger group. In small or larger groups they might stay for long periods in certain seasons at places where water and vegetation was plentiful or hunting was good. (The accounts of nineteenth-century white explorers in the western desert, and their helpless suffering from thirst, despite all possible precautions against it, highlight how wonderfully adapted the desert Aborigines were. What the white men did not know was how to tell, often by the length or colour of grass, or the presence of water-loving shrubs or trees, places where, if you dug a deep hole, it would gradually fill with water. They did not know either where to find deep cavities in rocks which might secrete water.)

The desert Aborigines had an elaborate vocabulary to describe a whole variety of water sources, from waterholes where water was nearly always available (big ceremonies tended to take place near to these), to small springs and wells that sooner or later dried up. Camps were usually within walking distance of some sort of water supply, and at each camp a group or family would spend several days before moving on.

Nomadism, even of a partial kind, makes it necessary to find temporary shelter, usually from the fierce heat of the sun in the case of desert dwellers. A grove of trees, or one tree, perhaps with branches from other trees propped against it or woven around it, was one solution. Several times I saw variations of this on shelters made with branches at Balgo – the older people still construct these for themselves and sleep in them during the hottest weather – and several times we came on such makeshift houses out in the bush, a sort of green cocoon.

In the very hottest weather, I learned later, the desert people travelled only by night, digging a hole in damp sand and sleeping until the sun went down. To reduce thirst, they covered themselves with sand.

In cold weather, by contrast, they found a natural windbreak, a clump of shrubs on top of a sandhill, where sand would gather. In wet weather, branches would be added to trees or shrubs or a hole would be dug underneath them. In the rockier parts of the desert, people moved into caves. Other shelters consisted of *kurrkuminti*, deep natural bowls in the sand, where whole families slept, with one or more fires to keep them warm at night.

The present-day people of Balgo seemed to live half in and half out of their houses, often using the house, at least in the hot weather, as a store room for their food and possessions, but living outside it, cooking over a campfire, even watching television across the campfire.

In the old days, there were no possessions to speak of – a few coolamons of different sizes to hold water or other food and liquid. They might have a 'plate' or two – a flat container, made out of tree bark – two grinding stones (a big 'mother stone' and a smaller one that fitted it, exactly like the querns used in Britain up until modern times) for grinding seeds for flour, a dilly bag or two of varied woven textures (the finest ones of all were said to be able to hold water), and sometimes some 'firesticks'.

For Aborigines, just like boy scouts, to make fire from scratch involves a wearisome process of rubbing woods together or sawing them in a way to make a spark. Instead, they invented the *jarra* or firestick. A stick of slow-burning wood was ignited and could be kept and carried from place to place, ready to start a new fire at the next camp. In cold weather it was a comforting source of warmth for the bearer.

The other valued tool of the women was the 'digging stick'; made of a hard wood, such as ironwood, with points at one or both ends hardened in the fire, it would be used to dig yams or other roots and tubers, to kill lizards and, by being pushed into their runs, to force small creatures such as rabbits into the open. I had watched the Kowanyama women use their sticks in this way to catch crabs.

Carrying their digging sticks, a coolamon and dilly bag or two, the women would set out in the morning to find food. As on the day we collected *tjunda* they collected vegetables and fruits according to season – there would be bush peaches and bush oranges, figs, plums or tomatoes. They also collected seeds, edible galls (from the mulga and bloodwood trees), tubers, roots, grass seeds (to make flour), grubs, nuts and small edible creatures – goannas, bandicoots, rabbits. Snakes would be held down with a forked stick and then killed with a stone.

The first goanna (large lizard) I saw was on the way to Sturt Creek. Out in the truck driving along the road, Helen and Ruth shrieked with excitement. 'Stop! Stop!' I could only see what looked like a bundle of straw on the sand.

Ruth and Helen were out of the truck like a shot and almost dancing along the sandy track behind the goanna as it made for its hole. Their total absorption in the task was infectious, as they found sticks to push into its run. 'It'll be in the pot before night!' said Sister Adele from long experience.

I never saw a snake caught, but it was regarded as a great treat. 'Python!' Ruth said, licking her lips. 'Python – just like chicken only better.'

Supper around the campfire is still the rule at Balgo. Nowadays they have knives, pots, pans. In the old days to cut food, as well as to perform many other cutting and scraping tasks, a white quartzite stone with chipped edges (very similar to ancient stone tools used in Britain) was used. Cooking utensils were made of wood, which made all boiling and stewing techniques impossible. Toasting, cooking in the embers or ashes or, in the case of large animals, putting hot rocks inside the carcase to speed up cooking and covering the outside of the carcase in protective material, thus making a sort of oven (just as I had witnessed in Kowanyama) were the ways the problem was overcome. Sometimes, too, cold food was warmed up by dropping a hot rock into the coolamon and moving it around. Snake was cooked rolled up, sometimes with the eggs inside. It is still cooked like that.

From about the turn of the twentieth century a few white artefacts began to make their way into the possession of even remote Aborigines, sometimes as a result of barter, or a chain of barterings, first from white man to Aborigine, then from one Aboriginal group to another; sometimes, probably, because objects were thrown lightly away by Europeans and saved by thrifty Aborigines. A common unconsidered trifle was a tin which had once held jam or other preserves. With a handle it made a billy, a cooking pot which could hang over a fire and heat water – Aborigines took up the new utensil with enthusiasm, particularly for the pleasure of making tea. Metal in other forms was also incorporated into spears and knives. Except in seasons of bitter drought the food-collecting of the women was pretty reliable and provided essential food that kept the group fed and nourished. It included a simple form of tobacco made from a shrub.

Hunting, largely a male activity, was a chancier pastime. Aborigines did not expect to have meat every day, so that a dish of, for instance, bush vegetables, or a simple bread or damper made out of spinifex seed (the well-known Australian camping food 'damper' was copied from the Aborigines, of course) might be supper after a hard day of exercise. To make the flour used for the damper might take hours of work. Spinifex seeds would be painstakingly cleaned of dust and sand, then the kernel would be winnowed from the husk and laboriously ground. It took an hour or more to produce a small cake the size of a saucer.

Grass, apart from providing a meagre flour, played a very important role altogether in the desert-dwellers' lives. In a way reminiscent of the wattle-and-daub method of building primitive British houses, grass was often used to hold mud or wet sand over a matrix of branches to make a 'house'. It also made a splendid thatch. Pressed into the seepage of a newly dug waterhole it acted as a filter against mud and dirt. Some kinds of grass were put into coolamons to stabilize the water when it was carried and stop it slopping, others were placed across the top of a coolamon or piece of bark to double its size by making a sort of nest to carry eggs or nuts. Carrying containers were made out of grass and, in the very hottest part of the year, when even hardened feet could be burned by the scorching sands, it could be plaited into a simple sandal.

A bunch of *jalngu* grass was used to improvise a simple spoon or dip known as a *mina*. A small twisted sheaf of dry *jalngu* could be dipped into honey and then sucked, or on a long journey, when water was scarce, the *mina* was used as a form of ration, wetting people's mouths and lips, but taking up very little water.

One of the most important uses of grass was to fire it. This could be an immediate hunting strategy, to flush out game: bush turkeys, perhaps, sand goannas or snakes. For a long time after such a burning, animal tracks were clearly visible, which helped hunting. *Jarra* were applied to the hummocks of spinifex.

Until a generation ago grass burning was an important task in the Aboriginal economy. At certain heights grass could help the hunter, but if it got too dense it became harder to find the prey.

Men's hunting took them over much larger stretches of territory at any one time than the women's. Just as there are precise words for different kinds of waterholes, or the different stages of the growth of grass, so there are many terms for tracks to be followed. After rain was a favourite time for hunting since it is possible to tell whether tracks are deep, or medium-firm, and thus predict the closeness of the prey. The tracks of the fastest animals – bush turkey, emu and dingo – are not much use. By the time the hunter has spotted them, the creature is already far away. Wild cats are more easily caught, having less speed and, more important, less stamina.

The emu, or *karnanganyja*, though fast on its feet, can be caught by ambush or cunning. Hiding close to a waterhole might give a chance to throw a spear as the emu drank. Sometimes the emu's curiosity would betray it. Lowe describes one man lying on the ground and kicking up his feet and behaving in a very unlikely human way.[1] The emu approaches to see what is going on and is speared by a hidden hunter. There was a widespread habit of steeping stupefying leaves in water where the emu came to drink – *tephrosia purpurea* or tobacco leaves in the desert. The hunter disguised his humanness with animal cries and gestures, and hid the smell of his sweat with mud.

The need to understand the particular habits and frailties of each animal seems to be the crucial skill for the hunter. Turkeys, for example, are so intimidated by fire that it is often enough to light a fire close to one to make it cower helplessly on the ground and become easy prey.

In search of such prey the men set off, sometimes for days at a time, carrying their spear and woomera, or spearthrower, knowing just when and where prey was most likely to be found. The spear would have a white quartzite flake carefully sharpened, and stuck to its wooden handle with *limirri*, a wax that came from the spinifex grass and could be turned into a strong cement. This was used, too, for the holder of the woomera.

The biggest game available to Aborigine hunters, so long as it was not their totemic ancestor, was the kangaroo.

There did not seem to be much hunting at Balgo except of small creatures perhaps because, unlike at Kowanyama, there seemed to be relatively few larger creatures now living in the surrounding desert. I never discovered quite why the desert itself seemed to be in decline.

The older people at Balgo had grown up in a world where the threat of hunger and thirst were part of their lives in a way unimaginable for most Europeans. Brian told me of one of the men who, as a little boy in the great drought of the 1920s, had been the only member of his group who survived.

'You never get over an experience like that.'

It helped me to understand something. It is possible to feel sadness for the grace of the old way of life, and admiration for its marvellous skills, yet see the irresistible attraction of a system which lets you buy food over the counter. Meanwhile the Balgo children still continue to learn many of the digging and catching skills, taught, it seemed to me, by their grannies rather than their mothers, the older women who still carry the old tradition in their memories.

CHAPTER SEVEN

On the way to the store, I was hailed by a couple of girls, Susan and Elizabeth, in their late teens, sitting on a kind of bandstand where the Desert Eagles, the boys' pop group, played in the evenings sometimes. The bandstand was a favourite hangout for the young in the late afternoon. Both the girls were very pretty: Susan shy, Elizabeth confident and bold.

'What your nem?' they began. The usual interrogation went on. Was I married? Did I have children? When we reached the entrance to Brian's house, Elizabeth said might she come in and have a cup of tea with me. Once inside she drank first lemonade and then tea, and then ate a large slice of a rather indifferent cake I had made from an instant cake mix bought from the store.

'Ah! brown cake,' she said. 'I like brown cake.' Then she came to what was probably the real purpose of the visit. Did I have a lipstick I would give her?

We were running out of conversation and an awkward silence set in. I felt the familiar frustration that it was difficult to discuss anything but superficialities. Elizabeth spoke English fluently, which I admired but, much like my own French, it did not extend to feelings or ideas. Or was it that I lacked the sort of human skill to draw her out on more interesting subjects – what she felt about life at Balgo, boys, marriage, her future?

Sensing the miasma of embarrassment, Elizabeth countered resourcefully with 'Let's draw!' At her suggestion we both wrote our names – Monica Furlong and Elizabeth Nakkamara Watson. Elizabeth then drew a butterfly beside her name, a spotted variety with long antennae, and drew an arrow from that to her name. With equal certainty she drew a flower in a pot beside my name but what, if any, significance there was in either illustration she did not say. Maybe seeing herself as a free-flying butterfly and myself as a flower in a container showed a good deal of awareness. Then she drew a tree, with a great deal of attention to its elaborate root structure, a bird, a snake, a boy, a guitar and a horse, in quick succession. Somewhere in the course of her drawing and chatting she remarked, 'Law truck's coming.'

I had now heard this slightly ominous sentence several times from a number of sources. I heard it first from Sister Cecilia, who had heard it among her students at the Adult Education Centre.

'What is the Law truck?' I asked Cecilia.

'They come round in a big truck and pick up all the young men for miles around to take them off for Law ceremonies.'

'What ceremonies?'

'Initiation and stuff. The women are not supposed to see the Law truck when it comes, so they stay indoors.' Cheryl spoke. 'They come into the clinic and say, "Don't go out, Sister. Law truck's coming."'

Brian, I discovered, was also concerned about the arrival of the Law truck. He was soon to take a party of men and women by truck down the Tanami to Alice Springs for a meeting of Aboriginal Catholics. Already the women in the party were beginning to worry that they might meet the Law truck on the road.

'Would it matter so much?'

'In the old days it was said that you were killed if you saw something you were not supposed to see. Nowadays, I don't think they'd kill anyone, but . . .' Brian shrugged.

Sister Adele said, 'It's like this every year. For weeks everyone is told the Law truck's coming. It doesn't come, and it doesn't come, but everyone is really anxious about it. The young men because they don't necessarily want to go with it, the women because they are afraid of accidentally seeing it. But it's not just women, it's anyone who has not reached a certain level of initiation.'

I at once remembered the story I had been told about Damian, a man in his thirties, a healer and one of Balgo's two rainmakers.

Damian was perfectly normal until about the age of seven when, accidentally, he heard, or saw, part of the men's ceremonies forbidden to the uninitiated. Nobody knew quite what had happened then, but since that day he had been dumb.

'Law' is a sort of shorthand word for everything connected with the life of ritual, ceremony, initiation and ethical practice. It arises, of course, from the Dreaming. I have the impression it is used more emphatically nowadays by those seeking to preserve the way of life of traditional Aborigines, that it is a word used almost as the antithesis of white beliefs and white law. Although its roots are in antiquity, or because its roots are in antiquity, it has become a unifying and strengthening force in re-establishing Aboriginal identity and self-esteem in a society that for so long despised and misunderstood Aboriginal spirituality and ethics.

As the fear around the Law truck reveals there is much about Aboriginal ceremony and belief that is secret; secret because it is so sacred that only the initiated understand it. It is felt that for anyone to come upon the sacred unprepared is to risk injury. Some places – often hidden caves – and some objects – paintings or sacred boards – contain too much of the numinous to be bearable for people not far advanced in spiritual understanding.

Aboriginal peoples grow up with many stories of the Dreaming which are specially important for that particular people because related to their 'country', or important because related to their individual totem. Everyone knows these stories – they are told around the campfire, scratched on the sand or on sacred boards, sung or enacted at certain ceremonies or, nowadays, painted on canvas. There are stories within the stories, sometimes relating to secret-sacred places. Boys at their circumcision ceremonies are taught some of the secret material. They see it danced, sung and acted before their eyes and they may not reveal it to women or to the uninitiated, on pain of, possibly, death. Women, once thought by male anthropologists to be excluded from this secret world, have their own Law from which men are excluded, and their own secrets.

The Dreaming – a way of seeing the world filled with numinous meaning, rather as some Christian mystics saw it – is about the way creatures and places came into being. The Ancestors, sometimes human, sometimes animal, sometimes interchangeably both, making their epic journeys, making love, fighting, resting, giving birth, transformed a flat, featureless landscape into a country full of sacred meaning.

Back in England I had studied C. M. Mountford's big collection of Dreaming stories[1] and felt a disappointment in the imaginative content, and a sense of puzzlement that they had such enormous religious importance for Aborigines. I think now that some of this had to do with a reverential approach in Mountford that somehow missed some vital spark in the originals. Recent tellings of Dreaming stories by Aboriginals themselves have a much more powerful quality. Sometimes they are deeply moving, like the story of the *luurnpa* as saviour given below. They reveal humour, irony (the latter, in my view, a sign of a developed culture), bawdiness. Always there is energy and life. Most of them imply a profound sense of the moral ambiguity of life – they are without the sense of the ideal one finds in Christian stories (though the Old Testament has a similar ambiguous quality). Though some of the stories have an Aesop's fables, 'stories for the kiddies' feel, in fact they deal with lust, incest, adultery, greed, the breaking of *tabus*, theft, and similar themes. They are, among other things, a pretty comprehensive survey of human failings.

Some of them, however, touch an even more basic human experience, that of survival. This is the story of the *luurnpa*, Balgo's totemic kingfisher, told by Gracie Green of Balgo.

> The People were thirsty, travelling north, down to the creek, where the tree was. The Kingfisher, he led them, he was ahead of them, the old man. He had a dog. The people were thirsty, dying. He brought the water to them in a stick in his beak from the place where the creek was. The Kingfisher brought them to the creek and settled them down there. Each time a person died, a tree grew. These trees are sacred, they are people.[2]

Gracie also told another Balgo story about how the Kingfisher took fire from the greedy Blue Tongue Lizard who kept it all to himself and gave it to 'his' people. The Lizard hid the fire in his head behind his ears or in his mouth (this gave him a blue tongue), while the People watched longingly from afar.

When the Blue Tongue was travelling, Big Bird, Kingfisher, dived down and knocked the fire from his head. He made all the fire come out of him . . . The Kingfisher knocked the fire out from between his ears, his tongue, feet and hands. Blue Tongue couldn't do anything. He was very tired and he said to the Kingfisher, 'This fire I give you.' He said that special trees would have the fire for men to make. Here a *coloom* tree, *gumbubano*, is the light tree, special to make fire.[3]

It is a feature of Dreaming stories that they happened right there in places known to everyone, and to people with names known to everyone. This is the Kukatja account of the Dreamtime – *Tjukurrpa* – as it happened to 'the People' in Kukatja country, and as it continues to be. It is about identity and sacred meaning.

A more general account of the Dreaming and the way it creates identities for different groups of people is given in Gracie's story of the Roughtail Lizard. It is perhaps the Aboriginal equivalent of the Book of Genesis, an account of origins, as when Adam names the animals.

A long time ago in the Dreamtime, there lived a Roughtail Lizard man who had a lot of Dreaming and songs he kept to himself. One day he was sitting by a waterhole called Ngamarlu, when some men, who were staying by the water, heard him singing.

Night after night those men got up to listen to that Roughtail man singing his songs as he sat by the fire. Every day when the men passed his camp they heard his singing. All the old people came together and they sat around, talking among themselves. They decided to send someone to meet him. 'Go and ask that Roughtail man to sing us a song,' they said. That person went over and asked him, 'Show us how to sing one of your songs.'

The Roughtail man answered, 'Certainly! I'll give you my songs to learn.' Then he called them all together and made them sit down and he gave to each man a song. He was putting white ochre on their chests, and saying to them, 'I'll give you this white ochre to put on your chests. All these songs are to be sung with ochre.'

One by one he gave each man a different song. Over and over he put the white ochre on them, telling them, 'This day I'm giving all these songs to the men. When I put this stuff on your chests, you may start to sing.'

Then he began singing for them and as he sang he showed them dances. When he had finished he said, 'I give these songs to the men to keep, each one in his own camp, a different song for each.'

And so from north to south, from east to west, each has his song from the Dreamtime. Today if you go over there to Wirrumanu you can see this waterhole called Ngamarlu.[4]

When the Sisters decided they wanted to go on a trip to Yagga Yagga I wondered whether they would be nervous of encountering the Law truck. They did not seem to be.

Sister Adele, Ruth Nakamarra and I set off to the outstation, a journey of about three hours, because Adele wanted to talk to them about setting up a clinic there. Rosemary, a visiting Sister with a wide knowledge of Aboriginal art, also wished to talk to a famous painter, Tjumpo Tjapanangka, who lived there.

Coached by Robin, I had placed a huge plastic container filled with water in the freezer the night before, so that I would have cold water for the trip. We set off at 7.30 and went up to the Aboriginal camp to pick up Ruth, immediately arousing a furious barking and chasing among the dogs. The 'camp' was a mess of plastic bags, discarded tin cans, an old iron bedstead and broken parts of cars, and the houses, simple prefabricated structures, looked uncared for, some of them with missing doors. The drive, like all journeys around Balgo, was one of moment by moment surprise and wonder. The track, and the conical ant-beds along its route, shone vivid rose-red in the bright sunlight, and the plants at the sides were a blue-green so brilliant that I felt at times as if I was hallucinating. There were mirages from the heat which added to the sense of reality dissolving. There was juniper, gum, oleander, bush potatoes and sometimes bright yellow flowers.

'Bush potatoes grow with rain,' one of the women remarked.

Most astonishing were the small flocks of budgerigars which would fly towards us at speed in perfect formation and then turn, suddenly, as they spotted us. As they turned, the sun glittered on innumerable emerald wings, and the beauty of the play of green light made me gasp. It felt like a moment of revelation.

With a thump the truck struck an unexpected pile of sand, and suddenly it leaped off the road and into the scrub at the side of it, imprisoned, hopelessly it seemed, in long grass, low shrubs and deep sand. We all tumbled out.

'At least we didn't roll,' Adele said encouragingly. 'Or hit an ant-bed. They can do an awful lot of damage.'

Ruth survived the situation hands on hips.

'You'll never get out of there,' she said with certainty. I felt gloomily she must know what she was talking about since this was her country.

She watched critically as Rosemary and I pushed the truck while Adele steered; the wheels spun in the sand, covering us both in red stains. Ruth laughed gleefully at this. With one final push, however, the truck suddenly leaped forward and Adele skilfully got it back on to the track. When we got to Yagga Yagga, we heard Ruth describing this incident to her relatives in fits of laughter, amusingly indicating our dismay as we got covered in sand.

The name Yagga Yagga means Quiet Quiet, and it was such a remote place that it was not hard to see why. Families at Balgo were all related to those at Yagga Yagga and were constantly coming and going between these and other outstations, staying with one another for days or weeks. There were some twenty houses at Yagga Yagga, none of them with water or electricity. We arrived as families were cooking their midday meal over campfires, big chunks of meat blackening over the flames. While Adele discussed the setting up of the clinic with a young white man – the husband of one of the Aboriginal women – who seemed to have a leadership role, and Rosemary talked to the famous painter, I crouched in the very small amount of shade left by the buildings. Some of the older women came up to talk and asked my name.

'My daughter is Monica,' one said in evident pleasure at the link between us. One of the old men mentioned to me that there were wild camels nearby in the desert and asked if I would like to go and see them. I was tempted, but not sure how long we were staying. I asked where the camels had come from and he gave a gesture of 'heaven only knows'. I wondered if they were descendants from Colonel Warburton's expedition, but no doubt other explorers or missionaries had imported them too.

In the truck we had speculated hopefully that we might get a cup of tea or even a bite to eat at Yagga Yagga, but no food or drink was offered to us. Rosemary tentatively asked if the store might be opened so that we could buy some food, but there was some suggestion that the key had been lost. Everyone was in midday stupor and had no intention of putting themselves out. On the long hot drive back I shared out the last of my polo mints and was glad of my water. I could not help remembering the generous hospitality of the Bedouin in Sinai and the way they offered tea, yogurt, cheese, halva in part, admittedly, as a way of holding visitors long enough to sell rugs, beadwork or silverwork to them. Certainly, after the nerve-wracking journey to Yagga Yagga, a cup of tea would have been welcome. I tried to find out from the Sisters whether this lack of hospitality was usual, but did not really get an answer. I tried out various explanations in my head: were they angry at our visit (but I did not get that impression), had poverty made even a cup of tea feel like an imposition? My guess was that it was rather that the white folk always seem to have everything, so it seems superfluous to try to share with them.

Rosemary had seen a Law painting by Tjumpo nearly finished, one that might be too secret for public display.

'No money, no finish,' he said, rather crossly.

On the return journey, Ruth promised to show us the place where two of the Ancestors, two goannas, I think (Ruth's description was confusing), had passed locally on their long journey to the coast, where they had cast two pearl shells into the sea. This event made pearl shells *tabu* for Kukatja women (though pearls were all right). Later I began to see that there were two basic kinds of myth. One, such as the one about the two goannas, was a travelling myth, one that covered a huge tract of country and crossed a number of tribal areas, the other was essentially a local story, related to the local landscape.

'Here!' said Ruth firmly, at a patch of desert that looked to us much like any other. 'This is the place!' We got out and stood looking out over the country, trying to picture the two goannas on their epic journey.

The stories, and the parts of the country in which they originally happened, belong to different kinship groups, and are repeatedly told or sung within those groups.

In other stories kinship or 'skin' names of the Kukatja figure prominently. There are eight skin names in all, so that each child born belongs in one of these subsections, and is required to marry someone from another 'skin'. A Dreaming story will describe some hero, or anti-hero, with one of those names. Not only are the mythical stories local but they are happening now to the degree that, through ceremonies and storytelling, people continue to invest in them. I found myself comparing this to the Christian telling of the story of the death and resurrection of Jesus in the Mass, and the Christian belief that Jesus is alive and relevant now.

Like all mythological stories, Aboriginal ones are on a kind of continuum between the undeniably sacred (say the Roughtail's teaching of the songs) and the secular or mundane (the innumerable Aboriginal stories in which people are punished for murder, incest, rape, or unfaithfulness in the case of wives). Yet there is not really a hierarchy of stories, good ones and less good ones; cunning ancestors like Crow who enjoy tricking, or naughty women like the wives of the White Cockatoo who cannot resist playing around with men are as much a part of the oral literature as the stories with deeper meanings. These sacred beings, unlike the Christian ones, are asocial and above the law. Like the Greek or Hindu gods they encompass all behaviour and all possibilities.

Nevertheless, a strict morality emerges from the beliefs, laying down an elaborate code of social behaviour, like whom it is proper to marry within a relatively restricted number of people. All human conduct is viewed through the window of the sacred.

In the west, we have split art from the sacred. In films, theatre, literature, painting, comments are made and forms of human conduct shown without reference to the sacred. This is necessary, since we now have no generally agreed view of the sacred but still have the need to reflect upon human conduct.

'Sacred' in Aboriginal language is a less abstract concept than it has been in the West. It is not mediated by a church, but by a direct awareness of the power in natural objects or landscapes. 'Believing' is about 'knowing', not making an effort to do something that is required. Outward conformity in ceremonies is all that is required of 'believers', not consent to a creed or to religious propositions. There seems to be no such thing as scepticism, simply the willingness, or unwillingness, to participate or invest in the important myths.

Unchangingness seems to have been the emphasis in Aboriginal religion. Passed on from one generation to another by oral transmission, as the stories and beliefs were, minor changes must have occurred. But continuity was the overriding intention, and this derived from the nature of the belief itself.

The mythical characters are not dead, but live on in the lives of humans who exist within the pattern. (Some of the mythical characters are thought to be literally the progenitors of the present Aborigines, others not.) Watching Ruth showing us exactly how the two goannas threw their pearl shells into the sea, I felt she might have been retelling a family anecdote about a relation whose story had been often told.

Yet it was also more than that; it was as if the subject of the story was acting it now. She was not just re-enacting the great journey of the goannas, but also recreating it. There is something opaque to modern white eyes in an experience like Ruth's. If the metaphor lives completely, it is no longer a metaphor – it is what it describes. In white consciousness, the times when experience transcends metaphor are rare, maybe growing rarer, and for some individuals perhaps the moment of transcendence never happens. If an Aborigine man says that a particular tract of land is his mother, he does not mean that it is like his mother. It is our failure not to know what he describes.

Our view of the world has been hugely influenced by its physical, scientific and quantifiable qualities. Aborigines are primarily interested in a quality of relatedness to people or to places in a kind of spiritual essence that is unquantifiable. For this reason, and for others too, material possessions have not, traditionally, been important to them.

Yet this has changed within a generation. At Balgo, the young men buy cars and are so proud of them that they will use them for the shortest journeys. The children often have bicycles. Clothes do not seem to excite much interest – it is simply too hot – and there are not many available. Television is part of the scene. One of the strange sights was a family sitting round a campfire cooking its meal while watching an American soap opera, full of American families, on a television set attached to a flex run out from a nearby house.

I felt an obscure disappointment that the old days of Aboriginal storytelling round the campfire – often illustrated by drawings in the sand – were being forced out of existence by the fantasies of Hollywood or white Australia. But then I could not help asking myself some questions. I am, after all, the owner of a television set (which I watch frequently), not to mention a VCR, CD, tape player and radio, as well as a computer, answerphone, vacuum cleaner, dishwasher, waste disposal unit and car. I enjoy my expensive toys and the sense they give me of participation in the world around me – its news, drama, art, gossip, etc. But just as radio and television in the West has killed off a good deal of conversation, amateur entertainment and individual activity, so Aboriginal communities will, of course, be affected by this powerful input of images from Western consumerism. Will it make them feel part of that world, or cruelly shut out from it? If they make sense of these images will it destroy the world they have kept in its unchanging essence for thousands of years? Or will they maintain their traditional lack of interest in possessions?

I am reflecting on a scene that has been repeated countless times in human experience – the scene where a powerful invader with a different world view overruns a community or country that cannot resist it, where innocence, in the sense of a wholeness of vision, is destroyed. It is tragedy and, unbearably, it is life. All of us, by the time we are adults, have suffered a destruction of innocence, from adults, schoolfriends, older brothers and sisters, as they pass some of their cynicism and aggression and greed on to us. This experience may make us gentler or more brutal in our attitude to others undergoing this primal disillusion, as we destroy innocence in our turn.

So is what has happened to Australia's Aborigines the same as, say, the Romans invading Britain and overwhelming the blue-painted Britons, or the white frontiersmen driving the native American Indians before them? In the nineteenth and early twentieth centuries it was very like the latter, and even now it does not seem to be widely understood how infinitely precious are the few indigenous peoples left in the world with cultures relatively intact.

The Aborigines, as Chatwin rightly said, are a tough and pragmatic people. The immediate effect of their growth in self-awareness in recent years, and of the movement towards Land Rights, has been to drive many of them towards traditional values rather than away from them, towards keeping the spiritual and human essence of communities like Wirrumanu at Balgo contained rather than dissipated. But the little box across the campfire offers powerful images of wealth and possessions.

CHAPTER EIGHT

One day, after a shower, I forgot to put my watch back on and after that I didn't bother with it again. Watch-time had become irrelevant.

Cheryl told me, laughing, about the day when Western Australia introduced Daylight Saving. At Luurnpa School the scheme was carefully explained to children and parents, and it was certainly mentioned to assistants at the clinic, students at the Adult Education Centre, and other workers.

On the first morning no one turned up at school until the usual time, in this case one hour late. Patiently and willingly, staff explained the theory all over again. People seemed to understand it and take it in, but on the second morning once again nobody arrived on time for school. If the sun is your timepiece and alarm clock to start the day then Daylight Saving is meaningless, one of those silly ideas that *kartiya* have, which are best ignored or treated with passive resistance. The idea was eventually abandoned. It came back to me how, as a child, I had bitterly resisted learning to tell the time and, eventually, only learned to do so under duress when the humiliation of not knowing what everyone else of my age knew grew too great. I just could not see the point of it.

Apart from using sun and moon as indicators of time, traditional Aborigines, like all people who live close to the land, described time by seasons: the cold time, the mild-weather time, the hot time, the wet time and the green-grass time. Particular constellations in the sky heralded certain events (or maybe produced them). When the seven Napaltjarri sisters – i.e. the Pleiades – appeared just before dawn in the sky it signalled the coming of the cold nights, cold because the sisters threw cold water upon the sleepers.

Time was often perceived also by a kind of deduction. When certain fruits and seeds ripened, then various animals came to eat them so it was hunting season. Mating seasons were important to know, particularly those of some of the lizards who got so carried away by their nuptial ecstasies that they could be picked off the ground without any resistance.

Pat Lowe describes the way a period of time was anticipated as if, for instance, a man was going away on a long journey.

> He would tell his family that he would be back with the first green grass and when the moon was full. They would then know almost to the day when to expect his return.
>
> Or, an older woman might point to the sky to indicate the position of the sun when an event took place. To her age group seasons still have more meaning than the names of months.[1]

Distance too, was very much caught up in the idea of time. The distance between two waterholes would be reckoned in days of walking, or a journey would be described in terms of the number of sandhills to be crossed.

A rhythmic sense of time certainly seemed to be invading me. As if I was sinking into a hibernation, the cyclic opposite of all my feverish Western activity, I grew sleepier and sleepier. I had wonderful nights – the soft rhythm of the fan soothing me as babies are said to be soothed by the rhythms of dishwashers and washing machines – and long sweet siestas, waking now and then to read a bit more of *War and Peace*, a novel which, a little oddly, I had chosen to sustain me with Western culture in this faraway desert. I realized with pleasure one morning that for the first time in months I had woken without a headache. Gradually, the dream of the night before came back to me, a dream of a huge, many-faceted jewel – perhaps a topaz – of great beauty. Nothing had happened in the dream; just the vision of the jewel.

I remembered another dream from ten years before in which I had got out of a train by mistake at a station called 'Headiam', realizing with distress that I had left my bag and all my important possessions on the train. It was pretty clear what it was saying – that I overvalued my mind and lost other important parts of me by doing so. I found this a rather humiliating discovery.

It took me several years to decide that this was not just my personal failure – though it certainly was that – but also part of the whole mindset of the west. What we have prized is what William James called 'directed thinking', the rationality taught by our education system, the finest fruits of which are science and technology. What we have downgraded, and what so many fine civilizations have prized, is the kind of thinking that emerges from 'spontaneous reverie': day, or night, dreaming. It has seemed to us archaic, the primitive thinking of a superstitious past, but in rejecting it we have lost touch with the primordial images, with the primordial sense of God and the sense of sacredness or numinosity which fills the world.

Searching for this shrunken side of myself I began to see the path that would be necessary, for me or for others, to recover that sense of sacredness. It was not about dramatic conversions or overt religion. It was about giving myself time and space to live more fully in the world than in my own head, to notice much more – plants, animals, people, places – to enjoy and marvel at them. So much seems to make that difficult: haste, worry, trying to make money, a longing for diversion. Those things take away the flavour of life, its meaning, its specialness, its taste.

One Aboriginal way in to the specialness of the world is through the totem. Just before a baby is conceived the husband, or wife, may have a dream associated with a particular place or a particular creature, or even a particular food, and that becomes the child's totem, that with which it will always have a special relationship.

At Balgo, unlike some other traditional places, unborn children are thought to live at sites important in stories of the Ancestors and these places decide the child's totem. A child grows up feeling special, in a sense 'chosen', because of its relationship to that sacred place, and it will probably dream about it. In several Aboriginal languages the word for 'totem' and 'dream' is the same.

The dream, and the totem itself, might be seen as a bridge across which those living in time can wander into the world of eternity. Even in the West we believe something a bit like this – it was Freud, after all, who described dreams as 'the royal road to the unconscious'. What is different about Aboriginal thinking about totems/dreams is that they believe eternal spirits move along the road in our direction.

Certain totems 'belong' to certain clans, or certain subsections, because of mythological stories associated with their 'country'. Others are more quirky and individual. The rain, the kangaroo, the crocodile, the firestick, the hairbelt, even vomiting, are totems. An individual may have one major totem and a number of subsidiary ones.

Maybe the most important thing about the totem is that it keeps open a fluid connection between humanness and nature, totally at odds with a Christian civilization which has not even believed that animals have souls. Aboriginal beliefs recognize that all forms of life share a commonality of attributes; all are profoundly related.

The special intimacy with the totem means that it may act as a helping animal or 'familiar' for a native healer. In ceremonies, the human being, copying the motion or habits of the totem, *becomes* it, rather as a great actor becomes his part.

Just as an actor has multiple identities – people with whom he has empathized to the point of 'becoming' them – so Aboriginal ceremonies enter mimetically or imaginatively into the life of a crocodile or a bird or whatever the totem creature may be, an extraordinary enrichment of understanding. This is possible because matter, nature, or animals are not despised as inferior to humanity but are seen to be as much part of the fabric of the sacred as ourselves.

Of course, in an environment where a deep knowledge of the weather, plants and animals is the key to survival, a close relationship with them is inevitable. At the annual 'increase' rituals, designed to facilitate the growth of plants or the breeding of animals, it is thought by Aborigines that the rituals are only successful to the degree to which one or more people present are in sympathy with both the subject of the ritual and also the Dreaming Ancestor, say the Black Goanna. It works, rather as we might say a performance of *King Lear* works, because of the attunement of the actors.

In a sense, the totem is a microcosm of the universe, a small scale vision – rather like the topaz in my dream – of the pattern and order and unity that runs through all things.

Totems also function as a link between people. Sometimes a whole clan will share a totem, possibly taken from a mythological event that occurred in their particular country. In the frequent cases where the Ancestors have travelled across country and their story is told by more than one clan or tribe, the same totem may be shared with others in distant places. These are 'group totems', totems in addition to the individual birth and conception totems described earlier. What is clear, apart from the extraordinary link the totem provides with the natural world, is that it creates a form of social adhesion, partly within the smaller groupings, partly within a much wider world of tribal division. In this it is not altogether unlike the role Catholicism has played in linking countries together across continents or across the world. Like everything else totems are sustained by a spiritual view of life, one rooted in *Tjukurrpa*, the Dreaming, in the myths of the Ancestors, in important rituals, and by important local sites – by 'country' or 'land'.

The rituals are mainly to do with matters in which human beings are most vulnerable: issues of life and death, fertility, and the relation between human beings and other aspects of nature. They are related to being part of a subsistence economy, directly dependent on the earth and what it produces, and on the animals, fish and other creatures which share that earth and its waters. For the Aborigines, it is a matter of life and death that the seasons should continue in an orderly, predictable way, that the supply of animal and vegetable food should not diminish. Farming communities in Britain until recent times, and probably in some places even today, showed vestiges of a similar dependence in fertility rituals, Rogation Days when God was asked for the weather needed to grow food, harvest celebrations to express thankfulness for what was given. The huge giant with his erect penis on the hillside at Cerne Abbas in Dorset was, for centuries, visited on midsummer night by women who wanted a child. (For all I know, this may still be the case.) In Aboriginal myth, the penis of the wicked antihero, Nirjana, gets separated from his body and travels around, chasing women, who then punish it by beating it with their digging sticks.

Perhaps the most widespread mythical stories which take many forms in different places are to do with the Rainbow Snake, always associated with rain or water. In some places, the snake lives in rock pools (and must be warned of the visitor's approach), and is to do with the rites belonging to native doctors or shamans. In Central Australia, he brings rain and spirit children. In other parts of the country, the snake is female, and associated with menstruation and childbirth, but also with bringing floods. In some versions, she is the first creator.

Certain objects are thought to contain a power or essence left over from the mythological time. Unless approached with knowledge and wisdom, this essence was dangerous, a conviction universal among traditional Aborigines. As with so many things I saw and thought about in the desert this idea seemed both strange and familiar. I remembered a moment of terror standing between two immense rocks in Cornwall when I was about thirteen. There seemed to me to be power there, a huge awe, which nothing in my background prepared me for. We are accustomed to little children or dogs or horses taking desperate fright at a place or a noise or even a person. As adults we use our rationality to protect us from this terror that the Greeks, for instance, who knew the possession of the Panic, were still in touch with. I suppose we might say that one reason we developed our rationality so extensively, our scientific awareness of 'how things work', was to protect ourselves from this primitive horror. It *is* good to have some protection from it, but if the price we have paid is to lose most of our empathy with the natural world and the feelings it inspires in us, then the price is too high.

One of the Balgo sisters described to me a mother coming to the clinic whose child had a stomach ache. 'What has she eaten?' was the scientific enquiry. Back came the answer, 'She wandered off in the darkness and something grabbed her.'

Here is a total mismatch of diagnoses. As Westerners we 'know' that what you eat affects the health and comfort of the stomach and gut. The Aboriginal response, however, begins from another place altogether. It sets the child, or the human person, in a total context of nature, and supernature, with all the potential beings, human, animal,

Ancestor and spirit that may help to shape it. It admits a great deal of terror (of the kind that generations of missionaries have seen as blind superstition), but it allows a world full of life and meaning.

CHAPTER NINE

The Law truck had come and gone, mercifully unseen by anyone who was not supposed to see it. It had taken some of the adolescent boys and young men with it, interrupting education, work, family responsibilities – nothing took precedence over Law business, the ceremonies of initiation.

'Do they always want to go?' I asked.

'No, sometimes they are scared and they run away.'

I wondered about women's ceremonies. Many of the first white people who were interested in Aborigines – many of them anthropologists – believed that the sacred ceremonies were entirely performed by men, with women banned from the scene or given a minor supporting role, cooking for the performers at a safe distance and joining in dances when allowed. It took the arrival of women anthropologists or, at least, the presence of the wives of male anthropologists like Mrs Meggitt to discover that women also enjoyed a ceremonial life of their own, though apparently a less dramatic one than the men's. At Balgo women had their own Law ground and their own ceremonies.

'Some women's ceremonies are very impressive,' Robin told me. 'At Port Keats when I was there the women went off for a fortnight together. At the end of the time the men prepared a huge meal to welcome them back. They waited and waited, and still the women didn't come. Then away in the distance was the sound of singing and we could see the women dancing as they approached. They were naked, painted up, beautifully decorated, and as they slowly approached, the men danced out to meet them. It was very moving.'

I had expected to learn that the ceremonies were dying as the white man's influence impinged upon traditional Aboriginal culture and induced clock-bound thinking. There *were* long years, in the late nineteenth and early twentieth centuries, when Aborigines living on missions and on cattle stations, on pearling boats and around mines, far from ancestral lands, felt their culture under severe pressure. For a while, it was generally believed that not only the Aboriginal culture but the people themselves might die out. Yet secretly, in deserts and stockyards, in defiance of priests and nuns and white bosses, ceremonies continued. Then, in the 1970s, there was a huge resurgence in Aboriginal confidence, and with it Aboriginal culture and religion – the outlook was radically changed. 'Law' became the way Aborigines sought to control their own lives and restore their damaged self-esteem. It was a way of defining themselves quite differently from white Australians.

Modern technology has slightly altered the old practices. The long walks between different camps, either as part of the training of a novice, or to pick up boys for initiation, or to meet up with clan members, have been replaced by cars and the 'Law truck'. In the vast spaces of Australia this brings different camps and tribes into much closer contact and perhaps makes for a pan-Australian Aboriginal solidarity. It lacks some of the poetry of the old walkabouts, the intimacy of knowing a country by walking it.

Some of the ceremonies remain, as they always were, 'secret-sacred', sights which it is a kind of blasphemy to witness without prior training and initiation. Those who are not initiated, or who are in lower grades of initiation, are excluded from ceremonies beyond their own level. White people are usually excluded from ceremonies, not so much because they are white (initiated white people are admitted) as because of their ignorance and incomprehension.

I noticed that *The Teacher's Handbook* of Luurnpa School felt a need to warn young white teachers arriving in Balgo that 'there is much in local Aboriginal tradition and law that is not told to non-Aboriginal people and the uninitiated'. Exceptions are those who have earned trust, partly by being able to speak local languages, partly by their love and devotion to Aboriginal people. Fr. Worms, for example, the anthropologist/priest who was one of the founders of Balgo, was allowed to watch secret ceremonies, and rumour has it that the present headmaster of Luurnpa School, Brother Leo, who had spent many years at Balgo, was regarded as 'not really a *kartiya* at all'. Sometimes the Sisters found themselves witnessing important ceremonies, ones where their safety would not be endangered.

In the very first long distance telephone call I had with Sister Adele, she described in some excitement the Balgo rainmaking ceremony to which she had just been invited. 'The young men were all painted up, and they had been fasting – no sex, no food, even no water, which was the greatest hardship because it is very hot at the moment. The older women came and with long branches dipped in water they sprinkled the men.' There was a pause, and then she said, 'It was like the Mass.'

What Adele was describing was an increase ceremony, a ritual designed to enable the workings of the natural world. The ceremony, held just before the Wet, re-enacted the water-bringing action of the *luurnpa*.

The ceremonies take many forms. They may involve visiting a sacred site and rearranging stones there, or painting them with red or white ochre; striking a tree and uttering a spell; calling out names or working on relevant cave paintings; opening veins and letting blood drop upon the ground; drawing a sacred design upon the ground with ochre, pipe-clay, blood, featherdown and other material.

These actions may be performed to make a particular bird lay, to encourage the growth of a plant or the breeding of an animal. For the ritual to work the performer (or performers) needs to be a descendant or reincarnation of the creature/Ancestor by means of the totem. This is what gives the ceremonies their power. Blood, or its substitute, red ochre, is very often used.

Some of the ceremonies are very simple; others are very elaborate and involve 'painting up big'. Some of them involve the *tjuringa* boards, which may be brought out of their hiding places in caves. Some ceremonies, particularly among women, are less to do with the Dreaming than with 'love magic', the attempt to enchant a desirable mate.

More important even than the increase rituals are the ceremonies of initiation of boys and young men, involving their circumcision or subincision. Not all traditional Aborigines practise circumcision and subincision, but in the Western desert boys undergo circumcision rites at puberty, somewhere between the ages of eleven and thirteen.

Parents and relatives decide that the boy has reached maturity, and they reassure him about what is to come. Alone or with other boys he will be taken to a secret place in the bush where he undergoes the first ritual which concerns a Dreaming story important to his family, designed as a revelation for him. He is placed under strict dietary rules – in particular, he is allowed no meat – and he is forbidden to speak more than is strictly necessary, using sign language to express his needs. He will be naked except for a hairbelt, his body rubbed with red ochre and fat, and his hair tied up in a top knot. Initiated men make a special design for him which will include Dreaming stories related to his family and his 'country'; and singing the songs, they paint the designs upon wooden shields which they then show to the boy and explain. There is dancing and singing, while the women of his family formally grieve over him. In the old days the boy was then taken on a grand tour of communities over a considerable distance, in the course of which he was taught about plants and animals, and about the totemic significance of natural features of the landscape. Ceremonies were performed at each camp, and the whole journey took two or three months.

At the original camp of seclusion a funnel-shaped ceremonial ground is specially prepared in the form laid down by the Dreamtime Ancestors. Dancing goes on for many hours while the boy lies on the ground covered by a blanket, not allowed to look or speak. Meggitt describes the Warlbiri pounding for hours on the earth to imitate the thudding of kangaroo tails. The novice is supposed to be absorbing the 'strength', the very essence of the songs.

Eventually, he is permitted to watch totem stories enacted by dressed-up, painted performers. He is solemnly warned never to reveal what he has seen, and there are suggestions that he will be killed if he does so. On the night of his circumcision, or ritual death, his mother dances with a lighted firestick which symbolizes his life. (Later, when he has been circumcised, she douses the fire to symbolize that her old son is dead.)

After many other ceremonies which emphasize his manhood, the boy is laid across the backs of relatives on a sort of table. One relative holds the shaft of the penis, another stretches the foreskin several inches, and another cuts it off with two or three quick slices. The knife used to be a sharpened flake of stone, nowadays it is more likely to be made of glass.

His brothers watch closely, for it is their duty to kill the operator at once if he mutilates the boy. (It is small wonder that some men are literally grey with anxiety when they perform their first operation.) The oldest brother inspects the foreskin, then throws it into the fire. Signals are given to those further away that the operation has been successfully performed.

The newly circumcised boy is praised by his mentors and stood in front of the fire where the warmth and smoke ease the pain. The boy has survived the 'little death' of severe pain passively endured, together with the fear of mutilation. The relief when this moment is passed must be very great. Although the moments of terror are all too real, the intention seems not one of cruelty but to impress a number of acts indelibly upon the adolescent boy. First, perhaps, the long seclusion, the pain, and the strange and unforgettable experiences of the ritual (unforgettable partly because of fear) make for a sharp separation between the child he used to be and the man he has now become. The many farewells and the mourning make it clear that he has left his mother for good, and that this is a kind of death. Second, he is now securely installed in maleness, and already knows the families from whom he may seek his future wife. Third, he is profoundly instructed in the Dreaming stories with which his family and his people are most intimately connected. He not only knows them with his mind but, as a result of the rituals and the deep feelings surrounding the whole occasion, he has absorbed and experienced them until he feels himself intimately part of the stories or the totem.

In addition to all this he is more tightly bonded to other men and to his people, with whom he has passed through so many emotions, and whom he has found it is safe to trust. He has a new relationship with his community.

In prospect a circumcision rite must be alarming, if also exciting. The Berndts, who watched circumcision ceremonies in the Great Victoria Desert, describe the attitude of boys they knew well as the time for the circumcision rite drew near.

Some . . . show a little uneasiness or nervousness; but apart from the fact that they have no choice in the matter, it has been pointed out to them that only in this way can they achieve adult status, be permitted to marry, and assume the responsibilities of family as well as of ritual life. Although most boys have vague ideas about initiation, they know virtually nothing of what happens until they experience it for themselves. The sudden awareness that this so-called ordeal is not far off alters a boy's whole approach to every-day matters. He pays close attention to the actions of his elders, in the hope that some slight unintentional sign or word on their part may give him a clue as to when he can expect it. He may also want to stay nearer his mother. Out-wardly, and especially to his friends, he may boast that the old men won't catch him, or that he is impatient for the rites to begin. In any case, even if he is afraid he is usually resigned and, in a way, anxious for the waiting to be over. If he has not been wild in his childhood, has listened to his elders, shown willingness and ability to remember what he is told, and if his spear is straight and his skill as a hunter is developing, he may not have to wait long for the first rite. But if the older men dislike him, particularly if he has been disrespectful or rude to them, he may be kept waiting for quite a while: or he may be more roughly handled during the actual physical operation . . .[1]

The circumcision ceremony over, the boy spends another week or so in seclusion, his hair being roughly, and painfully, cut off in tufts. He is allowed space to recover from his ordeal before he returns, not to his parents' home but to the bachelors' camp. His adult life has begun. Circumcision establishes his status among his people, his role in religious ceremonies, and his right to marry. No woman would marry an uncircumcised man. Meggitt says he only ever met one boy who had not been circumcised at the appropriate period of his life and he was mentally retarded.

Some tribes, in the desert and elsewhere, include other painful rites in the circumcision ceremony – knocking out a tooth, biting and gashing of the head or, in the case of the Aranda, pulling out a fingernail. The ceremony is indelibly fixed in the novice's mind both by the suffering, and by the knowledge that he has survived it.

There are other rites of initiation of greater or lesser significance – they go on up until middle age – but the next most significant one is that of subincision, a further operation on the penis, that takes place when the boy is around seventeen. Once again the decision is made for him by the men of his patriline. Once again he is secluded but not so strictly this time – he may go hunting with his sister's husband – once again he is covered with red ochre and wears only a hairbelt. Fellow countrymen and relatives attend the ceremony, which is much less elaborate. No women are present.

The ceremonies go on all night. Some time before dawn the youth's father and some others are decorated in order to enact an incident from the myth of their lodge.

As the sun rises, two of the men lie on their backs, side by side with their feet towards the fire. The youth is placed on his back on top of the men. The youth's penis is opened from the meatus to a point about an inch along the urethra which will make it broader and flatter. The operation over, its success is displayed. The patient squats over a small fire to relieve his pain and to help the blood to congeal.

Later in the day, female relatives who have been grieving for the youth's suffering may ask to be cicatrized in sympathy with him.

The point of the subincision ceremony is that a wound remains in the penis from which it is possible to squeeze blood, either to decorate a novice in a circumcision ceremony (blood is used as an adhesive to stick feathers, down, or other matter on to the body), or at a ceremony where blood is splashed on to novices (in some rituals they crawl through a sort of avenue of men standing with their legs astride). Many authorities have suggested that this is a symbolic imitation of menstrual bleeding.

The subincision ceremony is, however, associated with marriage. One side effect of the operation is that it makes the erect penis wider which is said to make coitus more enjoyable. Meggitt quotes Aboriginal women claiming that they would not marry a man who was not subincised. In theory, youths are not supposed to have sexual intercourse before the subincision operation and, if they are discovered doing so, the operation is performed as soon as possible. The young man does not have the marked change of status so dramatically brought about by circumcision, but he has become more eligible to have religious information disclosed to him and to take part in lodge ceremonies. When he finally approaches marriage, a couple of years after subincision, he is very much treated as a man.

Subincision, even more than the painful circumcision rite, is an operation which might well inspire fear in any man. Meggitt tells a story of a Warlbiri youth who was away doing stock work when his contemporaries were operated upon, and when he returned his kinsmen decided subincision was overdue.

> When his sister's husband escorted him at night to the creek-bed normally used for such ceremonies, his nerve failed and he escaped to the general camp. The men did not wish to pursue him and drag him away in the presence of women. The lad then camped close to the station homestead, judging correctly that the men would not try to seize him in the vicinity of the Europeans' houses.[2]

Later, however, when he thought he was safe and had returned to the main camp, nemesis struck.

> One evening in the bachelors' camp several of his sisters' husbands suddenly pounced on him and hustled him off to the creek, where the other men were waiting. His elder brother clubbed him in the back of the neck, and he was subincised before he recovered consciousness.

In this matter, nonconformity was not an option.

Other ceremonies in which pain plays an important part are cicatrization, not performed as ritual so much as a sign of bravery and manhood (possibly the use of the tattoo has played a similar role among some working-class men in British society), and because women are thought to find it attractive. At a lodge ceremony, two lines will be made in red ochre above the nipples on the subject's chest with a flake of stone or glass. Men press the edges of the wounds apart and fill the incisions with down and sand, blowing on the wound to ease the pain. The scars will be raised. On a later occasion, a man will have another two cicatrices added on his chest and may have as many as eight or ten. He may also have cuts made on his shoulders. Summer is the time for this because there is less pain than in cold weather. But there is a strong admiration for the ability to withstand physical pain – it is a sign of adulthood and of manhood. Another practice of the southern Warlbiri was to pierce the septum of the nose with a sharp stick, so that adornments could be worn there during ceremonies – a bloody and painful operation.

For Westerners, particularly for men, stories of initiation have a fascination. Women anthropologists have suggested that male scholars and writers have given them an undue importance in the overall pictures, claiming that they had an obsession with them which distorted their studies.[3] Whatever the slanted view of male anthropologists, there seems little doubt that circumcision is a key ritual, and one in which women play a strange (and minor) role, resisting the boy being taken away, mainly in a form of play, but also resisting, probably with deeper feeling, the loss of their child, as their son leaves to become a man.

In Aboriginal culture, as in so many others, the ritual of puberty for girls is menstruation itself. When menstruation begins a girl goes into seclusion some distance from the camp and often practises food *tabus*. Older women may join her to teach her songs and myths. She will later return to camp beautifully decorated and painted. As with the boy becoming a new person, there is some sense that the girl is a new woman. Some tribes have a ritual of breaking the girl's hymen, which is seen as a sort of equivalent of circumcising the boy. Others, more distressingly, have a ritual form of gang rape, which is supposed to prepare the girl for marriage but probably terrifies her. There may be rituals for the growing of breasts, customs of piercing the septum, or cicatrizing. A girl is being prepared for marriage – she may practise love magic to be sure she gets the man of her choice – and this will lead to birth. I wonder if childbirth, following on a few years after menstruation, does not represent a kind of equivalent of subincision – a severe experience of pain and revelation on the threshold of adult life. These two inescapable experiences for women – of menstruation and childbirth – perhaps prescribe the two-stage male initiation with its more artificial infliction of pain. Growing up is, for both, a clearly marked rite of passage.

The ceremonies bring about a clear differentiation of female and male. The circumcision ceremony with its male bonding, the emphasis on separation from the mother, its pride in the penis and the power of the male, seems a reminder to the boy of the way he needs to go, relinquishing femaleness, finding his future in the male role. Perhaps the ceremony recognizes that the psychological pain of the choice is considerable and needs to be represented by the severe physical pain he endures, but he is shown that there are compensations – male friendship, status, religious knowledge and, eventually, marriage. In the subincision ceremony there is an odd hint that on the far side of maleness freely accepted, femaleness may be rediscovered, in this case by an imitation of menstruation.

For the girl, nature arranges the drama.

As in so many parts of the world, the ceremonies show a recognition of the power of women, along with many stories of power being taken from them. In the desert near Balgo it is said that in the mythical era women possessed all sacred ritual, only to have it taken by men. Among the Aranda, too, the same story is told of former equality and possession of sacred emblems. In the Great Victoria Desert, Ancestral Emu women are said to have taught the art of circumcision, replacing the dangerous method of the firestick with the better one of the stone knife. In Arnhem Land it is said that the Kangaroo Man invaded the women's camp while they were dancing, drove them out, took their sacred emblems, and began copying their motions and songs with his friends because they had none of their own.

> The men had taken from them not only the songs, and the rituals, but also the power to perform sacred ritual, a power which had formerly belonged only to the Sisters. Before that, men had nothing. The elder Sister said ' . . . Men can do it

111

now, they can look after it . . . We know everything. We have really lost nothing, because we remember it all, and we can let them have that small part. Aren't we still sacred, even if we have lost the baskets . . .?[4]

CHAPTER TEN

One of the pastimes of white Balgo was Scrabble and a couple of times Anita asked Robin and myself over for supper and a game. These small social events were good fun and I found myself looking forward to them. On these occasions, or driving together in the truck, we talked a lot about the job of being a nurse at Balgo and what Anita felt about it. I was struck by her lack of sentimentality. Certain things could be done about people's health problems at Balgo, other things could not be done. There was a kind of acceptance which was, perhaps, the only way to live with the disappointment and frustration that, despite enormous hard work, Aboriginal health was still so bad. I questioned her about her sense of vocation – she belonged to a Catholic order of nurses who, while not nuns, had taken a vow of commitment to the work that included celibacy. The commitment was to work with disadvantaged people.

'Does that mean that if you met a man you liked you couldn't get married?' I asked.

'That's right.'

One day a week Anita set off in the truck for Billiluna so that she could 'do the clinic' there, and I asked to accompany her. Elizabeth and Caroline asked to come too to visit their relatives. 'Actually, I think it's their boyfriends they want to see,' Anita said.

Billiluna had been cut off from Balgo since the Wet, the sandy track that passes for a road having been washed into the deep waters of the creek. The road was still officially closed to all comers and I knew that the truck would have to run through deep water at Sturt Creek with the chance of getting bogged down.

We had been driving for perhaps an hour along deserted tracks when we arrived at the flooded creek and found a huge bus stuck firmly in deep water in the middle of it, making it impossible for anyone else to pass. Anita remarked that the creek crossing was deceptive – the entry to the water which seemed shallowest led into the deepest part. To cross you had to drive down a steep bank into what appeared to be deep water, after which the water became shallower almost immediately and you were on firm ground.

She jumped out of the truck, walked to the edge of the stream, and stood gazing at the bus, hands on hips. The bus was a long-haul tourist vehicle useful for the Australian distances, with sleeping cabins for passengers built into its high sides. A number of passengers – German, we discovered, most of them rather elderly – sat disconsolately along the roadside in clothes unsuited to the desert, without shade, in a sun that was already mercilessly hot. They looked curiously at us and at our Aboriginal passengers.

The driver was still fruitlessly trying to get the engine to start. When he eventually emerged from the driving cabin, Anita shouted angrily, 'You've really stuffed up the creek! Didn't you see on the signs this road is closed?'

She sauntered back, winking at me as she passed, muttering, 'Don't mind my Australian!' and with superb economy of manner she leaned into the back of the truck and brought out a long pole – a wireless mast. Nonchalantly, she screwed this on to a pole on the front of the truck, took up a microphone, and before an admiring German audience gave her 'C Charley Tango' calling sign. It was answered and she summoned help. It would take several hours to arrive and there was no point in waiting since we could not cross the creek. Anita cancelled the idea of Billiluna for that day. Elizabeth and Caroline were unwilling to accept her reasons. The plan had been to go to Billiluna and they were still determined to go. They said they would walk the rest of the distance. Anita said it was too far and that she was responsible for them. They argued passionately that they must get to Billiluna, but Anita kept pointing out that she could not get there for hours, she would rather postpone it for another day, and that she could not leave them.

They lapsed into talking sulkily to each other in Kukatja. Five minutes later as we were returning to Balgo along the red tracks, they shouted 'Sistah! Sistah! There is a man!'

'A man?'

'By the road, asking for help.'

'Where?'

'A way back. A way back.'

'Why didn't you say?'

'We say now.'

In the desert, there is a strict law of caring for one another – it is easy to die because of a broken truck, no water, or because you are lost. Anita turned and we drove slowly back the way we had come, almost as far as the creek and the German truck, scouring the sand and the bushes for the needy traveller.

'He may have been dead!' said Elizabeth, dramatically.

'I thought you said he was asking for help?'

'Or ill,' put in Caroline. 'There was a woman screaming and waving her arms!' she added improbably.

'Well, he'll have to manage without our help,' said Anita at last, as the German truck began to appear in the distance.

'Oh, Sistah, let us down here. We can walk from here.'

The ruse didn't work. Anita turned the truck again and sped back to Balgo, the two girls grumbling all the way.

Next time we went to Billiluna the creek was clear and Anita performed the unnerving manoeuvre of driving over the steep bank and heading straight into the water. The water washed around the middle of the doors, but the truck found track beneath its wheels and soon we were pulling out on the other side of the fast-running water.

Billiluna was one of the oldest outstations and I thought the prettiest, with a softer and cleaner look than Balgo and many more plants to soften the bareness and the isolation. The Flying Doctor taxied down the airstrip as we got there, in a small plane advertising the Argyle Diamond Mine. First a handsome young male doctor in shorts, then a smart woman doctor and a nurse all emerged from the strip, just like in a Flying Doctor film. I had asked if I might consult a doctor, and I got the handsome young man.

'It's dizziness,' I said, describing rather frightening balance disturbances I had been experiencing when I got out of bed or even stood up after sitting down. He diagnosed a mixture of low blood pressure and dehydration – the hot climate was affecting me more than I knew.

'Nice meeting you,' he said. 'I mostly work with people who can't tell me their symptoms, and it certainly makes the job easier when one of them can!'

I asked him about the symptoms he usually dealt with and he told me the story I had already heard of malnutrition and poor hygiene: 'sores, skin problems, bad eyes, ears, diabetes, heart trouble, the occasional snake bite'.

Sitting waiting in the clinic I noticed the sort of posters you see in GPs' waiting rooms in England, warning you of this, or encouraging you to do that. These posters offered nutritional advice and among the foods recommended were kangaroo, emu and snake. I thought what an extraordinary contrast the clinics made with traditional Aboriginal medicine. Like clinics in the Western world they offer special help to pregnant women and to babies and children, as well as to the elderly. The older women at Balgo remember a different way when, accompanied by a grandmother or other older relative, a woman in labour would choose a sheltered spot in the bush where she would be gently massaged throughout the birth. The umbilical cord would be cut with a piece of sharpened quartz, and the baby gently cleaned all over with sand. No man would be present at the birth but the father and other relations would encourage the birth with song, maybe assisted by a native doctor, and they would perform certain ritual gestures aimed at 'easing'. In the old days of a generation ago, it was a life where there was little 'expert' intervention, at least in the areas where modern people feel a need for professional help – birth, death and illness.

The local knowledge of herbs produced medicine for local ailments. On the coast, for instance, morning-glory leaves were used to relieve the pain of jellyfish stings. Again on the coast, where arthritis and rheumatism were a problem, a warmed bundle of the dodder laurel gave comfort. The warmed leaves and stems of the desert walnut also alleviated rheumatism, and an infusion could be made for skin sores. In the Kimberley, the snake vine was bound around the head to relieve headaches while the burning resin of the spinifex grasses was used to make smoke which was a headache-relieving decongestant. Wood-smoke was also thought to be helpful, for this and other ailments. Certain acacia smoke was thought to be healing for sores and for women recovering from childbirth. Stems of the vine were used as splints for fractures and as a mosquito repellent.

The Walmajarri painter, Jimmy Pike, remembered the life of the people of the sandhills in his childhood as one of good health. 'Most of the ailments from which the desert people suffered were the result of injury, such as burns, cuts or insect bites. People sometimes had headaches, and occasionally children got a condition known as *Yama*, in which they were covered with distressing sores. Any injury would attract flies and might become infected. A few people suffered from weeping ulcers which would not heal. People treated . . . cuts and sores with *kiyimi*, the reddish-brown sap or gum that bleeds from certain eucalyptus trees when they are cut.'[1]

A coating for cuts or bad burns was a mixture of *mungju* – antbed – and water. Applied as a muddy paste, this would dry and form a type of plaster. It was most often used to cover the injuries people inflicted on themselves at times of bereavement, when they expressed their grief by striking their heads with boomerangs or rocks.[2] In hot weather, it was sometimes applied to babies' heads as a sort of sunhat.

Acacia was used by chewing the leaves and applying the juice to burns. 'Bung-eye', the miserable condition when the eyelid swells as a result of a bite, was cured with crushed leaves and saliva. Human urine was used both as an antiseptic and also as a medicine for gastro-enteritis. Drinking urine can be a remedy for dehydration.

Measles, mumps, chickenpox, smallpox and the 'cold sick' were all brought to Australia by Europeans, and the Aborigines were quick to work on new medicines to combat these scourges, using the newly acquired metal 'billy' to allow them to boil plant infusions and so achieve more concentrated solutions. The 'cold sick' – *kungkurr* – was treated by giving the patient a pungent root bark to suck. Like many Western medicines for sore throat, it tasted nasty and gave a burning sensation which seemed to relieve the symptom.

More recent sickness in the desert comes by sexually transmitted disease. It puzzled the Sisters that Balgo women were becoming pregnant much later than was usual in traditional communities, or not becoming pregnant at all, and gradually STD was suspected. More frightening still was the prospect of AIDS. Already down at Alice one or two cases had been reported. 'We have always said that whatever happens at Alice sooner or later happens here. In this case we pray to be wrong.'

It felt wrong that a people so gifted in the use of natural medicines, and traditionally so self-reliant, were now so dependent on Western medicine and needed the intervention of white people to help them to deal with their illnesses. At Balgo and, as I later discovered, in the cities of Australia, doctors believe Aborigines cannot be trusted to take antibiotics or other medicine regularly: 'They'll only give them all away to their relatives!' This meant that, unlike white patients, Aborigines have to return every day or two for supplies or, at Balgo, be visited at home by the Sisters.

The irony is that, in addition to herbal knowledge, Aborigines have had a long healing tradition of their own, performed by native doctors, or 'clever men'. These still existed and played an important part in ceremonies such as rainmaking, and they were undoubtedly still called upon to perform acts of healing, probably alongside white man's medicine.

Brian remembered a day when a Balgo man had had a severe case of snakebite. 'The Sisters bound it up tightly, I think with a tourniquet, to stop the poison spreading. Damian [the rainmaker/healer] came in, and wanted to take the bandage off and suck the poison out. Of course, that used to be the Western treatment for snakebite, and I wonder if he was remembering that, or whether he had his own method, but because he can't speak I couldn't ask him, and now we'll never know.' Brian sounded wistful. 'I'd sort of like to see Aboriginal medicine and Western medicine slog it out. But of course the Sisters insisted on their way, and you can't blame them.'

For Westerners, healing has become a profession practised in isolation from religious and spiritual beliefs (though this was not so in the beginnings of Western medicine), but for the Aboriginal 'clever man' – *maparnpa* in Kukatja (there is also a word for a 'clever woman', *minyara*), healing was only one aspect of a life given up to a particularly close relationship with the supernatural.

Studies of shamanism in many parts of the world suggest that shamans were either eccentric and strange from childhood, or that they suffered some childhood trauma of great severity that marked them out from their fellows. (This idea persists in the Western idea of 'the wounded healer'.) Carlos Castenada, in his probably fictional but nevertheless convincing portrait of a Mexican Indian 'sorcerer', Don Juan, reports the violent death of Don Juan's parents before his eyes as a child. Damian, the mute shaman of Balgo, had clearly been traumatized as a child. Perhaps the key is a sense of isolation, for which consolation, a sense of meaning in life, must be sought at a deeper level of awareness than the mundane. It is also true, however, that among Australian Aboriginal shamans, there is a tendency for the role to be passed down in families, rather like a profession. Whether or not the job is inherited, it is usual for the shaman to have had a mentor, either his father or another shaman, with whom he has studied and to whom he has acted as assistant. Thus there is a kind of 'probation' period before he embarks on a magical career.

Neither personality, nor family background, are the whole story. If the average young Kukatja man is expected to undergo the initiation of circumcision and subincision, the shaman has to experience all this and much more. The disciplines of shamanhood lie on the far side of the rites of manhood. They are, as it were, the Ph.D.s of the spiritual life.

This raises some questions about the women shamans referred to by a number of scholars – there did not appear to be one at Balgo. Since women were excluded from the male initiation process and so could not have passed the preliminary 'degrees' necessary for male shamans, it must have been assumed that as women menstruate, give birth and participate in female rituals, they are qualified for the higher training. When it comes to matters like magic or healing, people are more likely to judge by results than formal qualifications, and some female practitioners were undoubtedly gifted with 'powers'.

In the parts of Australia where circumcision and/or subincision were not practised, one of the paths of shamanic vocation was a deep trance or vision in which the visionary might discover a special awareness of the 'sky heroes' or Ancestors. This was known as 'putting, or going through, the rule'. In the places where circumcision was practised the process of becoming a shaman was like a deeper experience of the circumcision ritual itself, that is to say it was a form of death or 'being killed'. Ordeals, nearly always experiences of loneliness and fear as well as pain, took place at special waterholes, places belonging to the Rainbow Snake who has an affinity for healers and shamans. Perhaps the most important thing about a shaman was that he/she learned to commune with the spirits of the dead, or at any rate was able to see them without being overwhelmed by the experience.

The 'death' that the postulant underwent might include being left alone for hours in places where the spirits are active; having magical paraphernalia (crystals, for example) inserted into the scalp or the arms; having 'operations' performed on the abdomen (sometimes literally, sometimes metaphorically) so that 'new insides' can replace the old ones, or the old ones be cleaned and replaced. Other rituals take the form of spirits removing the postulant's mind and replacing it with another mind. The significance of this is that the shaman symbolically dies and is resurrected. With the incisions and removal of organs, it is also rather like a mummification process. The assumption is that the death and rebirth involve a transformation process so that after it, enlightened by a mystical process, the shaman has new powers, and a superhuman strength, at least of a psychic kind.

The powers vary widely between different individuals, who tend to be gifted in specific ways. But, overall, magic tends to come in three kinds. There is productive magic, increase and fertility rites, rainmaking and love-magic; there is protective magic, either healing or counteracting misfortune or accident; and there is destructive magic intended to bring sickness, injury, and death. Many shamans move between these 'good' and 'bad' aspects of magic.

Perhaps by embodying the interrelatedness of all the manifestations of nature the shamans have a more important function than the magic itself. The shaman may be a visionary, foretelling and shaping the future actions of the group. A shaman's understanding is expected to be above, or beyond, more far-sighted than that of more ordinary mortals. They will almost certainly perform a healing function, using rites and spells, herbal remedies, ventriloquism, sucking techniques and certain magical objects such as crystal, bones, stones, etc. They may have special diagnostic ability. Trickery, sometimes of a kind that is easily seen through, is noted by those who have observed these doctors, yet this cannot be quite what it seems. Native doctors, well aware that tricks are used, do not hesitate to consult each other when they need help.

Many shamans have spirit familiars, connected with their totem. Shamans, reputedly, can change into animals, fly, travel at extraordinary speed, or become invisible. They can make rain, or divine the identity of a murderer.

Their most feared function is of 'singing' or 'pointing' a person, casting a fatal spell upon them that brings immediate sickness and death, a custom also well known in Africa. In fact, in the age of witchcraft, European witches were often accused of pointing.

Wanting to injure a victim, the shaman concentrates on him and may observe *tabus*, for instance, by fasting, to prepare himself. He visualizes the victim intensely, and transmits the thought of fatal sickness, perhaps in the form of a bone in his inside, perhaps in the favourite way of 'having his kidney fat stolen'. There are methods of doing this, and prescribed words to be said. The 'implement', the pointed bone or whatever it may be, is merely the outward declaration of destructive intent.

Apart from pointing, a number of terrifying devices are used by sorcerers to inflict sickness and death upon victims. There is 'magic powder' made either from the dust of a corpse or from a placenta which, sprinkled upon food, causes slow or faster death according to quantity. There is 'image sorcery', known within our own witchcraft tradition, in which an effigy of the victim is pierced, and a variation of this in which the likeness of a person is drawn on a stone and the stone is heated in the fire until it breaks. This is performed in Arnhem Land and is said to turn the victim into a leper. A portrait of an unfaithful wife or her lover may be used for black magic in this way. But the shaman who knows how to point also knows how to counteract the effect of pointing. Those who suspect they have been pointed need to find a powerful magician to save them.

Sometimes pointing is done by using an object that has been in contact with a victim – say the leavings of a meal or faeces. This particularly virulent form of pointing is used on the Lower Murray River, and huge psychic strength is expended by the shaman in concentrating on a victim with hate and wishing him to die. '"Let the life-breath leave thy body, O boy! Die!"'[3]

These frightening accounts of pointing raise an interesting question. Is it only those who believe in this power who are affected, whose minds have been trained to fear this kind of intervention, or can the 'ill-willing' damage anyone? This is particularly relevant in the Aboriginal situation. Bitterly oppressed by white invaders, often miserably exploited and sometimes actively persecuted by graziers, cattle-station owners, pearlers, miners and others, why did they not use this secret technique to get their revenge?

I know of no hard evidence of their having done so, though there are vague stories of their having used magic to produce bad weather to plague white farmers, and of curses against white folk being passed down from generation to generation in certain families.

It may not be only belief that causes pointing or singing to work on an Aboriginal or African victim. Telepathy is extraordinarily powerful, and it is claimed that it can be used to attract the attention of someone standing some distance away. I did not see this happen, but several anthropologists testified to its working.

In communities where people are closely attuned to one another and able to share ideas without spelling them out in words (not unlike the way some couples are able to do), a capacity that must have been very useful in the fast and incalculable demands of hunting, it does not seem surprising that either supportive or destructive thoughts could be exchanged. An interesting insight into this capacity appears in *The Teacher's Handbook*. In a description of a repeated classroom situation, written by an Aboriginal teacher, it depicts a form of communication that must be bewildering to white class teachers.

> Aboriginal children use their bodies, their hands, their ears, mouth, head and nose more than anything else. If they talk, they only use the key word. Say if you ask them 'Where is Bobby? Tell him I want him,' they relay the message to where Bobby is, by only using Bobby's name.
>
> Or you might be in a classroom with the children working quietly and all of a sudden somebody cries. You ask what's wrong and the child that's crying will say, 'Johnny's teasing me.' Then you think, 'Now, how did that happen?' because you know the class had been quiet and you didn't hear Johnny call the child that's crying any names. But

Aboriginal children use different parts of their bodies to get a message across.

A child has ringworms on his body and the other children know he doesn't like being teased about it. Someone in the class might attract the attention of the child that has ringworms, then he looks quickly across to the map of the world or a globe and the child automatically follows his eyes and ends up crying because ringworm reminds the children of the map of the world.

There were two boys, and one boy's father had a name that meant that he had something to do with the sky and the other one fish or fishing line. One of the boys started doing actions as if he was fishing and the other one kept looking up to the sky.

They kept this up for a while and then the boy said to the teacher, 'There's a lot of fish in the river, when can we go fishing?' and that did it, he made the other boy cry.

Looking at someone from the corner of your eye means he wants your attention or what you're telling isn't true.

Poking your tongue out of the corner of your mouth means you're a liar.

Tapping the crown of your head with the palm of your hand means swim.

The shared imagery and an approach to life that is more visual than verbal makes for subtle forms of mockery, and also a form of vulnerability that, unlike our own teasing, depends little on words. This can be used by the shaman for his own purposes.

Like so many 'clever' or 'holy' men and women in many parts of the world, the Aboriginal shaman can, it is said, perform inexplicable deeds (often at circumcision ceremonies, either to impress other shamans, or to awe the initiates). He may be able to roll in fire or walk over it without getting hurt. In south-eastern Australia, he has a 'magic cord' sung into him as part of his initiation. This cord is then used to climb up into the sky, or to float up and down horizontally.

Other tricks take the form of appearing and disappearing, of dissolving into a tree, of travelling at extraordinary speed, of running phenomenally fast without losing breath, or of running a couple of feet above the ground. Some shamans claim that the air moves, carrying them with it. It may be, of course, that these incidents are examples of mass hypnotism, but it still seems remarkable to create the illusion. And, in fact, mass hypnotism seems an inadequate explanation of some phenomena.

> W., a doctor (shaman), was with some other Aborigines at the horse-yard on a station where they were working. When the rest set out for the camp, a quarter of a mile or so away, he remained at the yard, saying he would catch up with them. When, however, they reached their camp, he was sitting there making a boomerang, as though he had not been away. They did not see him pass, and there was no hidden track by which he could have hurried around.[4]

Whatever the awareness of the Aborigine and the *maparn*, it emerges from an experience of great tranquillity almost unimaginable to Europeans, the absence of all rush and sense of urgency, a condition in which the mind is deeply receptive to the psychic. The shamans, and probably most Aboriginal people to some degree, are accustomed to engage unselfconsciously in what we, selfconsciously, describe as meditation. Many shamans, in particular, specialize in a form of deep recollection, sitting down by themselves in order to 'see'. This seems to lead them into a clairvoyance outside our understanding.

The power is thought to be present in everybody, but to be especially developed by only a few. Apart from the *maparn* and the *minyara*, old people are also said to have some gifts of 'second sight', perhaps because their lives are less stressed than those more actively engaged in pursuits.

It is the vocation of some shamans to entertain the spirits of the dead and to see visions of the living. In some parts of Australia it is said that shamans may ritually eat part of a corpse in order to commune with the dead and reap the knowledge and power of this awesome experience.

Noting the similarity of many of these shamanic practices and phenomena to those noted in Tibet, some anthropologists (A. P. Elkin for one) suggest that Aboriginal spirituality and shamanistic practice may have anciently come from the same source. It is certainly Oriental, rather than Occidental, in many of its attitudes and ideas.

Love-magic is an important part of the shaman's repertoire. Since this seems to interest women particularly, maybe it is this in which women shamans specialized. In the deserts around Balgo, it is claimed that women's secret ceremonies related especially to love-magic. Body painting, and the use of particular ornaments, would be forms of magic designed to attract the person desired. Since some of the love-magic songs (of both men and women) seem related to stimulating sexual interest, it seems possible they were a way of overcoming shyness or fear and bringing young lovers together, though it is hard to see where stimulation ends and magic begins. In Arnhem Land there is a method of drawing a picture of the person desired having sexual intercourse with the subject, which is said to attract them, though the picture must be touched up from time to time to hold their interest. In other cases, special rites are performed to restore the failing love of a partner.

Magic, it becomes obvious, comes into its own where deep imperatives are involved: rain and increase of crops and animals, all of them essential for survival; relief of sickness and pain; coming to terms with death; obtaining love, a sexual partner or a wife; and revenge where deep wrong is felt to have been done. It feels oddly familiar not only because our own culture still has vestiges of harvest magic and love-magic. The corn dolly and the Harvest Festival (dating back to the nineteenth century as an established church service, but part of a much older custom of harvest rituals), the prayers for rain in the Book of Common Prayer, take us back to a period, perhaps not much more than a hundred years ago, in which people literally starved in a bad year. Customs of throwing an apple peel over one's shoulder before going to bed on Midsummer Eve, so that the initial it suggests reveals one's true love, the use of love potions and aphrodisiacs and various techniques to see into one's romantic future, bring us very close to the shamans' love-magic, and take us back into our own tradition of witches and magicians.

Most of us, *in extremis*, find ourselves resorting to what we might call 'superstition', or, more acceptably, religion, praying for recovery, help, or reciprocated love.

CHAPTER ELEVEN

On Sundays I went to Mass – I wouldn't have missed either the singing, or the sight of a church full of naked and naughty children, for anything. On weekdays too, I sometimes went to the evening Mass to which only whites turned up. It was an informal service. People sat round in a circle, suggested subjects for prayer and, occasionally, got into discussions.

On St George's day, Brian remarked, 'Isn't George the patron saint of England, Monica?' I agreed that he was, and went on to describe that extraordinary place at Uffington where some say George killed his dragon. I described the white horse on its dizzy hillside, the hump at the bottom (the dragon) with its chalk eye gazing heavenwards, the deep red scars on its sides (the dragon's blood), and the legend that nothing will grow in the fields around it.

'In fact, a Dreaming story?' said Brian. It came as a shock – the shock, repeated again and again as the weeks went by, of discovering that Aboriginal life was, in important ways, familiar, similar to much I had known before.

I was curious both about how the original Catholic missionaries to the Kukatja had seen their role, and also how Brian and Robin saw theirs. A number of the first missionaries to the Kukatja people were Germans, members of the Pallotine Order. One of these, Father Francis Huegal, took over a cattle station homestead at Rockhole, south of Hall's Creek, in 1934, with the intention of establishing a leprosarium. (The first death from Hansen's disease among the Aborigines had occurred in 1908 and, by 1936, there were two thousand cases, many of them among the Desert Aborigines). The Government refused hoped-for funds.

In 1939, Father Alphonse Bleischwitz travelled south with sheep, camels, and horses and was joined by a small group of Aborigines in a succession of temporary camps. After many adventures, including the priest's internment during the Second World War, a more permanent site was found at what is now known as 'Old Balgo', about an hour away by truck from the present site.

When I asked about Old Balgo one hot lazy Saturday afternoon, one of the Sisters said, 'Let's go. We'll see if we can persuade Gracie to come with us. She's the person to tell you about it!'

Gracie, a Walmajarri woman now in her mid forties, was born at Billiluna, and is famous in Australia, like a number of people connected with Balgo, for her writing, painting, and sculpture. She was sitting out in the afternoon sunshine looking after her grandchildren and, without any reluctance, was persuaded to hand them over to another relative and come and join us in the truck. 'We want to go to Old Balgo, but we need you to show us the way.'

For part of the journey it was the usual bumpy ride along a sandy track, avoiding ant-beds and ruts and, then, dramatically, Gracie pointed across country, and we left the track and set off over sand and scrub. It was hot and very bone-shaking, the flies were as busy as ever, and I began to struggle with my old disability of car-sickness. My attention was distracted by the extraordinary sight of three beautiful black foals running away from the sound of the truck. They had the grace and nervousness of racehorses.

One of the priests of Old Balgo, I learned, came from a well-to-do, Irish racehorse-owning family. He had the inspiration of using Balgo to breed horses, partly to make money, partly as a livelihood for Aborigine men, and he had horses shipped out from Ireland to help with his scheme. It had not worked, I am not sure why, perhaps because Old Balgo suffered from a chronic shortage of water, but some of the descendants of the fine Irish stock had escaped, and continued to breed in the desert. 'Sometimes, in a hard year, they die of drought or hunger. But mostly they manage to survive out here, and now and again they are rounded up and sold.'

I found it hard to believe that Gracie's very definite and peremptory instructions, 'Turn here! Go across there!', could possibly get us anywhere in a landscape that seemed almost without features but then, gradually, a ghost farm of blackened wood, tumbled brick and broken cattle fences, rose before us. Gracie stood in the middle of it and pointed. She had been six or seven when, in the mid-1950s, her Mum and Dad had brought her here and left her. That was where the girls' dormitory had been, there was the convent, there the chapel, there the priest's house. We stood beside the empty well and looked at a landscape ravishingly beautiful in its colour and distances and its gentle contours, but as remote as anywhere on earth. I wished I had seen it buzzing with life.

It had been a small community. In 1956, the 'Johnnies' (Sisters of St John of God) joined the Pallotine fathers, set up the school for Aboriginal girls and also offered some medical care. By 1959, the whole community numbered sixty people.

Buildings were made of stone and clay and wood, and there was a large brick oven to bake bread. Fruit trees and a vegetable garden were planted, and there were farm animals, but the community was not quite self-sufficient. Fuel was needed for a generator which supplied a meagre flow of electricity. Water was always a problem.

In addition to reading and writing, Gracie had learned cooking and housekeeping from the Johnnies and, on Wednesdays, all the girls worked in the laundry, washing clothes by hand.

'Were you happy here?' I asked Gracie. Her face was expressionless.

'Good. Good school,' she said. I sensed that she felt things she was not saying. Blocking my question saved her from expressing what may have been complicated feelings about Old Balgo. Undoubtedly, she felt some loyalty to her teachers and her old school, and why should she trust me, a virtual stranger, with criticisms that might be damagingly used? Or was it simply that explanations did not interest her? Most Westerners feel that it is possible to be critical of teachers and schools years after the event, but Gracie was not to be drawn.

In 1963, partly because of water problems, and partly because of lease problems, the Balgo community moved seventeen kilometres to the new site, called both Balgo and Wirrumanu, where beneath the sand and rock there was an inexhaustible supply of artesian water. This blackened scarecrow was all that remained of the original Balgo.

128

Much scorn is now expended on missionary history in Australia, some of it by Aboriginals themselves, some by white writers and campaigners angry on the Aboriginals' behalf. Hearing even Gracie's relatively benign story, it is easy to be critical of these pious incomers who, ignorant of the superb domestic economy of traditional Aboriginal life, could not rise imaginatively beyond teaching Western cooking and housekeeping. Later, though not from Gracie, I learned that *corroboree*, that important coming together of Aboriginal groups to meet, dance, and enact ceremonies, was forbidden at Balgo until 1969. It was thought best for Aborigines to forget traditional ways and acquire European habits, probably from an unimaginative conviction that Western ideas and ways were superior to all others. The priests thought in terms of providing men with work – cattle-breeding, horse-breeding – and the Sisters in terms of making good housewives. (But also of curing the horrors of Hansen's disease, and other dreadful scourges of illness.) As so often when thinking about Australian history one feels caught in a net of pain, some of it caused by brutality and greed, but as much by poignant and repeated misunderstandings.

It was in Brian's library that I read about the work of the man who was perhaps the ancestor of the new kind of missionary, the kind who was fascinated by and respectful of traditional Aboriginal life and belief, as Brian, Robin and Philip each were. Father Ernest Worms had a scientific education, was wounded as a soldier of the Kaiser in the First World War, was a Pallotine, and was ordained priest in 1920. He studied ethnology and linguistics before becoming parish priest of Broome in 1930, and he saw that part of his work as priest lay in immersing himself in the customs, beliefs, rites and mythology of the Aborigines. (In the late 1920s there had been a sudden upsurge of scholarly interest in Aboriginal life in Australia, and it was recognized that the Kimberleys were one of the few areas where that life was still more or less intact.)

Apart from his deep fascination with the Aborigines, and his gentle tolerance, Worms had an insight of crucial importance. It was that much missionary teaching represented a failure to face psychological realities, in particular the reality that though mission-educated Aborigines might appear to be dutiful Christians they did not, in fact, abandon their own deeply experienced beliefs, nor their ancestral practices.

What he thought was precious, what Aborigines had in abundance, was *faith itself*. The Dreaming, it seemed to him, was a flame of spiritual vitality that, once extinguished, could not be rekindled from another source. Above all, he saw that identity and self-esteem were inseparable from belief, and that even if the Christians had the power to dislodge Aboriginals from their ancient beliefs, which they did not, to try to do so was, however unconsciously, a desperately destructive act.

What is moving about Worms's thinking is the reverence and awe, the perception of the importance of the enterprise that he brings to Aboriginal rituals and beliefs; in his time it was not so easy for a Catholic father to bring this breadth of understanding to a culture so different from his own. Above all he had a vision of human unity, of the extraordinary similarity of experiences everywhere upon earth that kept the human experiment in motion. The techniques he had to learn to help him to understand Aboriginal beliefs showed him, in spite of himself, the increasing onesidedness of European thought, its emphasis on rational thought at the expense of the deep wells of primordial experience.

In 1937, Worms became very interested in the Kukatja people, still living in the old way, many of them still never having seen a white man. He approached them with infinite courtesy and delicacy, making friends of one or two members of the tribe and travelling with them, setting out, according to Mary Durack, with 'water-bag, billy-can, pannikin, camera, notebook and a few iron rations'. He walked along the Canning stock route, 'the longest and loneliest track in the world' that ran east from Hall's Creek, the only track locally penetrated by white men, where one or two white stockmen had been speared. But Worms, known to many Aborigines as *Ibala* – the 'learned elder of the tribes' – was welcomed at campfires by the Kukatja, where he watched with the deepest interest both what was eaten and how it was prepared. 'On one occasion, presented as a special delicacy with what looked like a type of nut, he had no sooner put the kernel in his mouth than it disintegrated into a mass of wriggling maggots. The 'nut' was a hardened exudation of sap from a tree strung by some astute insect to form a hatchery for its eggs!'[1]

Worms continued to work on his writings about Aboriginal life and particularly to study Aboriginal spirituality, as he continued to work on his knowledge of Aboriginal languages. It was he who selected the site of Old Balgo 'about seventeen miles south of Gregory's Great Salt Sea and some fifty south of Billiluna'. His understanding spirit continues to reign at Balgo Wirrumanu to this day.

The Catholic presence there certainly seems different from the old missionary ambitions. *The Teacher's Handbook* describes the original function of Balgo, innovatory in its time, as being to 'provide a buffer between the traditional Aboriginal way of life and the new life on the cattle stations where the Aborigines were under the control of European settlers'. Two reasons were given for this, one that the Aborigines from the desert had been forced out of some of their old food-gathering areas, as the Australian army moved in and established ammunition dumps in the desert during the Second World War. The other was the constant availability of food and water to a people who had frequently lacked both.

The power base changed fundamentally at Balgo during the 1980s when, following Aboriginal wishes and Federal Government demands, the Catholic Church formally handed the Balgo mission over to the Aboriginal community, to be run by the Aboriginal Council. Henceforward, white people were employed at the discretion of the Council. When I was at Balgo, there were ten of these (to about five hundred Aborigines): Brian and Robin, the two Jesuit priests; Health Centre staff – provided or paid for by the Sisters of Mercy; teachers in the primary and Adult Education Centre; and an art organizer, who arranged for the supply of canvases and paints to Aboriginal painters, and the sale of their work to the world outside. The Kukatja tended to think of themselves as Catholic (and to find no apparent conflict between this and Law). Brian and Robin remained key figures within the community. Brian spoke enthusiastically of this. It was entirely in keeping with the undogmatic way he wanted to work.

'One thing,' Brian said to me one day, 'celibacy is absolutely incomprehensible to them. Since family is everything here, and sexuality is a very natural and straightforward part of people's lives, it puzzles them that anyone should be deprived of these things. I've never found an adequate way of explaining it to them.'

Brian's thoughtful, undefensive statements became my principal way of interpreting the world of Balgo. I felt that he never stopped

131

trying to see the best way to do his job, to see how he might be useful to an Aboriginal community becoming more and more determined to stand on its own feet. In an unassuming way he was a constant resource for everyone. Two or three men would drop in to discuss some dispute with him, sometimes coming and sitting in the kitchen to talk over a cold drink, sometimes standing uneasily outside until he joined them there. Sometimes a woman with a drunken husband who beat her would call. Sometimes several of the young men would drop in to strum on his guitar.

He led a fairly austere life (not by Aboriginal standards, but by the standards of most urban priests), as he had for twenty years, far away from interesting white contacts, fresh food and most of the amenities of civilization. He had a TV set, however, and a supply of exciting video films. He was tough, physically strong and practical, unsentimental both with himself and with the Aborigines. He set boundaries.

The refrigerator in the kitchen always contained a jug of lemonade for droppers-in – offering a cold drink in the fierce desert climate was, for Brian, the natural courtesy. Since alcohol was off-limits, drink treats were Coke, Fanta and similar soft drinks which he allowed himself and Robin at nights when they were watching *The Bill*. Aboriginal visitors had a way of rejecting the lemonade and asking for Fanta. Brian feigned the most wonderful indignation. 'When I come to your house you don't offer me Fanta. When you offer me Fanta, I offer you Fanta.'

It took me a while to work out that what Brian always did was to establish equality of responsibility. The only time I saw him angry was when one of the Sisters told him about a man who had come to the Sisters' house begging for food for his wife and family, which they had given him.

'But he's working and getting paid,' said Brian.

'Well, he didn't show up for work this week, so he didn't get paid. So they couldn't buy any food.'

Brian shook his head in rage and astonishment at the Sisters' softness. In his eyes they had demeaned the man, reduced him to a kind of 'native' status.

'I suppose they were worried about the children going hungry,' I said naively.

132

'In this community?' Brian said, sceptically. 'Their relatives would never let that happen.'

He was also dubious about the ramifications of health care given by the Balgo clinic, with its refusal to place the responsibility for sensible drug-taking in Aborigines' own hands.

'How can people learn if you don't treat them as grown-up people? There's nothing stupid about these people.'

'It must be hard,' I said. 'If you think a child might die if it is not given its drugs regularly . . .'

'So a child dies?' said Brian. 'Maybe that is the only way to learn about medicine.'

It was harsh, but a harshness born out of deep respect and love.

'Is it lonely here?' I asked him once. 'Don't you wish you were in a town somewhere?'

He considered.

'It's just about all right,' he said, 'if too many things don't come at once.' (He meant fights, disputes, accidents.) 'If there's time to think, to pray, to study the language, then I'm okay.'

On another occasion, he said it was the older women who helped him through.

'They are really very loving, and they care about me. Some of them, strictly speaking, should not be speaking to me, nor I to them [he meant that his 'skin' relationships to some of them actually forbade conversation]. 'Fortunately they are prepared to make an exception in this case. I'm not sure why, and I don't ask.'

It was through Brian that I learned how the Jesuits of the Northern Circuit in Australia had thrown themselves vigorously behind Aboriginal Land Rights. Frank Brennan, son of a well-known Australian judge, and himself a lawyer as well as a priest, had directed UNIYA, a social research and action agency aimed at the long, painful process of 'reconciliation' between Aboriginals and white folk. He was a long-term adviser to Aboriginal communities on land-rights matters (and, as such, a thorn in the flesh to many whites) and advised the Australian Catholic bishops on Aboriginal matters. Brian himself had spent several years researching on behalf of the Royal Commission into Black Deaths in Custody. A group of other Jesuits – moral theologians, systematic theologians, social scientists – had lent their strength to Aboriginal arguments.

On the wall in Brian's kitchen was a slightly amusing photograph of 'all the Jesuits in Australia', as Brian put it, a group of about a hundred men of different ages and colours (only two of them wearing a Roman collar, I noticed, the rest in casual wear). It appeared to have been taken from an upstairs window, which gave them an oddly fore-shortened and slightly sinister look, like the sort of almost-human in a Hollywood film about aliens. It did not flatter them.

The anthropologist T. G. H. Strehlow, by no means uncritical of missionary endeavours in Australia, nevertheless made the startling claim, that 'the missions were the only agency that held up the complete physical annihilation of the Aboriginal race in this country from the beginnings of white settlement till the time when more enlightened Government policies were instituted in Australia.'[2] Despite Christian bigotry and narrow-mindedness, repression and ignorance, there was also a sense of human dignity and worth, and a devotion and love, however misguided at times.

Like Strehlow, I was moved by the Christian work at Balgo, as I had been moved by it at Kowanyama. Christian blindness and bigotry has done more than its share of harm in white relations with Aborigines, but the present generation of missionaries, humbly nursing, befriending and facilitating a proper recognition of Aboriginal gifts and achievements was impressive, perhaps the innovators of a new respect and tolerance in the field of religion.

CHAPTER TWELVE

It was not until an art dealer from Sydney, Adrian, arrived in the company of a writer-friend, James, that I fully realized Balgo was an important centre for Aboriginal art. Adrian, a practising Jew, was obliged to spend Passover in the unlikely setting of Balgo, and he had complained to his grocer, as he packed up the necessary food, that he would have to observe the occasion alone.

'Nonsense!' the grocer had said. 'There are Jews everywhere!' And sure enough, a young Jewish teacher at Luurnpa School had been happy to celebrate with him.

Adrian and James brought in a breath of the outside world, and I was delighted when they asked me to have supper with them one night. Unthinkingly, I followed their example and drank wine with my steak – the only alcohol I ever consumed at Balgo. It did not occur to me until I was talking to Robin afterwards that I had broken one of the few strict rules of the place.

Remembering the art gallery at Perth, I began asking Adrian about Aboriginal paintings and, quite quickly, began to realize that through art the mythical and dreaming world could be studied, and the barriers of language and of different concepts could be partly overcome.

There were, of course, different schools of Aboriginal art. Different tribal communities had different, though often overlapping traditions, all of which included some sort of painting – sand painting, rock painting, painting of the body. The geographical distances between communities were often vast, which encouraged 'inclusive' forms of art to spring up. Apart from this, many of the painters had been exposed to Western influences – to missionary schools and churches in particular – which influenced both themes and style.

The Arnhem Land 'X-ray' artists, like the painter of my emu picture, worked exclusively in strong desert colours and materials – red and brown ochre, charcoal and white pipe-clay. The north Kimberley painters produced huge haunting rock pictures of *Wandjinas* – white spirits with big eyes and no mouths. The Balgo painters, in contrast, had a much more 'geometric' and pictogrammic style, painting their landscapes with circles (often indicating waterholes), footprints (of animals and people), wavy lines indicating dreaming tracks or creeks, and different colours indicating bush foods. Though some had worked mainly in ochre in the past now, like many other contemporary Aboriginal painters, they worked in colour using a multitude of spots to build up shifting expanses of colour with a mystical intensity. What the writer Judith Ryan, speaking of the work of Tim Leura Tjapaltjarri, called 'a veiled prism of soft light. It is a world in which Dreamtime past, present and future are held in balance.'[1]

Sometimes the effect was like a *pointilliste* painting, though a non-figurative one. It seemed like a map, or an aerial view, revealing the relationship of one topographical feature to another – a 'camp', a creek, a waterhole, a fire, tracks where an animal had walked maybe dragging its tail behind it like a possum. Or so I thought, but Adrian had a different, more interesting idea. He suggested that it was a view of the land painted from *underneath*, from, as it were, a position of total immersion within nature.

It was Adrian who taught me that the brown horseshoe shapes were a cipher for people sitting on the ground, often round a campfire. (I sat down on the sand at once to experiment, and yes, my bottom and thighs did make just that shape.) And he explained how the dots were an extension of body-painting, when 'painting up' a man or woman might dip a thumb in the paint and ornament themselves or another. There were obvious links too with the sand paintings in which a picture, outlined with sand, might be filled in with kapok, leaves, or seeds, making up a mosaic effect. Or with more modest works of art on an occasion when a parent or elder might tell a Dreaming story round the campfire after supper, drawing sketches in the sand, of the route the Ancestors had taken. The use of circles and concentric lines recalled the incisions on *tjuringa*, the sacred boards. Ceremonial art found its way on to even the simplest canvas.

Together Adrian and I went into the Art Centre at Balgo and looked at canvas after canvas in shimmering colour, paintings that were both abstractions and yet also very much 'of' particular places – Dreaming tracks, mythical stories, or simply pictures of a favourite desert location. Here, in return for paints and canvases given to them by the art organizer, members of the Wirramanu community painted their pictures, and had them sold to the occasional knowledgeable dealer, such as Adrian, who visited this remote place, or shipped out to dealers in Sydney, Melbourne, Perth and Darwin.

Behind this sale of their work was a moving story, the story of what became known as 'the Desert painting movement'. In the past, Aboriginal art, at least in the central desert, had had a purely ritual and religious purpose, as perhaps all art did in its earliest origins. In 1971, quite suddenly, something different began to happen.

At Papunya, 250 kilometres into the Western desert from Alice Springs, a young teacher, Geoffrey Bardon, was placed in charge of art teaching at an Aboriginal settlement. He had been appalled at what he found there, much later describing 'the sense of horror' that still overcame him when he remembered a place where 'the human dignity of Aboriginal people was held in utter contempt', a place of 'degradation, disease and filth'.

In the 1960s the Commonwealth Government had planned Papunya as an Aboriginal town where remaining nomads could be brought in from the desert and receive education and a chance to be assimilated into mainstream Australian life. At Papunya, as elsewhere, it did not work like that. It produced, Bardon says, 'constant unrest and a breakdown of Aboriginal social order, chronic health problems and the highest infant mortality rate in the world'.[2]

He describes his first impression of the place as one that 'always looked desperate through its wild red dust: a vague, ramshackle coming-together of ugly corrugated-iron transitional huts, stilt houses, a hospital, a white-painted school and a police station. It had graded symmetrical streets without names, and barbed-wire fences in front of each house. There was a small desolate red patch of parched sand in front of each house for a garden. Mostly I remember that strange

desert settlement as a silent and oppressive convergence of red hal-
lucinatory white-people's roads emerging from the surrounding
spinifex and acacia desert, to stare at that lost settlement and then to go
sadly on . . .'³ Most of the Aboriginal population lived along 'rutted
roads in terrible galvanized-iron shanties'.

The people were a mixture of desert tribes. There were Luritja,
Warlbiri and Anmatjeri Aranda who had worked for white people,
often as cattlemen, and now were too old or ill to continue. Their
white association had, ironically, protected them from some of the
worst massacres and degradation, and their own tribal sense had
remained strong and in part intact, though their traditional way of life
had been taken from them. There were also Pintupi – the 'wild
Pintupi', Bardon calls them (they were among the last to have contact
with white people) – who had been forcibly brought in from the desert
in 1962, and who had no wish to stay at Papunya. No one was allowed
to leave without government consent.

Papunya was, in fact, if not in name, a penal settlement, run by white
people who were not so much brutal, as totally without comprehension, feeling or respect for Aboriginal values and beliefs, and who kept
Aborigines there rather as animals have often been kept in a zoo. The
gulf between black and white was almost total, with no attempt at any
kind of social mixing, with the inferiority of the Aborigines, even in
the desert where they knew better how to survive than their white
keepers, absolutely taken for granted. Bardon makes the shrewd observation that he was never quite sure whether the Aboriginals were
protecting the whites from the desert, or the desert from the whites.
But the race of warriors and hunters were now reduced to crushing
boredom, and the inevitable despair and drunkenness of those for
whom life has no meaning.

Then something happened that was eventually to affect all the desert
Aborigines, an extraordinary rediscovery of creativity in the hellhole
that was Papunya. It was an explosion of art, what Bardon calls 'an
incandescence which in 1971–2 became a great artistic and spiritual
conflagration among the desert tribes.'⁴

It began in the school where Bardon tried to get the children to
paint, not the imitation of Western art so often taught in the mission
schools, but traditional Aboriginal designs and patterns that he had

repeatedly watched them scratch in the sand. The school classrooms were mounted on steel columns with bare, unpainted walls between them. Bardon hit on the ambitious plan of getting the children to paint murals on the walls. The task went slowly, the children not really warming to the task. But the school yardmen asked to join in, and gradually the pensioners, gardeners, and other local workers were involved. At some point, the project really fired their enthusiasm and the traditional designs began to take their place in Dreaming stories. Then one particularly gifted painter among them completed a magnificent mural of the Honey Ant Dreaming.

It had seemed to Bardon that the misery of Papunya stemmed partly from exile, but also from the loss of all sense of 'glory' – the glory there had once been in hunting and the great mythological rituals. 'The glory, as I came to understand, surged forth in the immense, almost desperate creativity of people seeking only to be themselves.' There was 'a visionary power' with everything done 'wildly, lovingly, exultantly, so as to change forever that desert world.'[5]

Bardon eventually left Papunya but, by 1980 when he returned, the old settlement was disappearing, by fire, hooliganism and white disinterest. He reflected 'how those white people in that brief time in 1971–2 believed they had made this now-ruined town, in a visionary but trivial pause, before that enormous desert returned irrevocably to itself.'[2] But Papunya, or at least the art movement, had done its extraordinary work. Within a few years the incandescence had spread all over the vast central desert area – Kukatja, Warlbiri, Luritja, and Pitjantjatjara – were all painting, depicting fragments of song cycle, religious and ritual knowledge. Their tribal identities, so threatened by the white invasion, particularly for those who lost their traditional land, were strengthened, their children were educated by the paintings in their own tradition, and the task itself re-enlivened them. Almost miraculously, it must have seemed, it brought money to poor communities which lacked paid work, money which increased as soon as 'acrylic' Aboriginal art became known and admired by those far from traditional Aboriginal communities.

Because the subjects are so often linked to religious and mythological meaning, the selling of work is not without serious difficulties. Unlike the old cave and sand paintings, works on canvas, which may depict secret-sacred themes only meant for the eyes of initiates, will be seen wherever they are displayed or sold. This caused distress at Papunya itself where, in that first outpouring of love and longing, the implications of the content were overlooked at first, and it has caused problems around Aboriginal art ever since, probably exacerbated by the indignation of activists in the cause of Aboriginal rights. It is rumoured that all the major art galleries of Australia now have rooms full of Aboriginal paintings too secret-sacred to be shown publicly. But partly because most people who look at the paintings will not be able to perceive the deep meanings which would be obvious to initiates, and partly because it seems possible to draw a rough distinction between 'permissible' bits of Dreaming stories and the impermissible parts, there are now many paintings which appear to offend no one and yet which, often in their extraordinarily ecstatic quality, hint at what is unseen.

In 1986 an exhibition of Balgo art – *Art of the Great Sandy Desert* – was shown at the Art Gallery of Western Australia in Perth, and was immediately acclaimed for its strength and quality. Painting began at Balgo in the 1970s, undoubtedly affected by the Papunya movement, since some of its artists had lived at Yuendumu, near to Papunya. At Balgo, as elsewhere, there was doubt and anxiety about painting for a *kartiya* audience. Balgo was more cut off from outside influences than many other places by its geographical isolation. There was, however, a Catholic influence there, with painters such as Matthew Gill Tjupurrula finding inspiration in Christian themes, as paintings in Balgo church demonstrate to this day. Without completely ignoring Catholic ideas, however, the heart of Balgo painting was and is traditional Aboriginal belief, pictures of Dreaming stories, of 'tracks' and 'country' precious to its people. Some of Balgo painting is still secret, performed as ritual body paintings, sand drawings and rock paintings, and such work would be done largely in the 'sacred' medium of ochres. The use of acrylics or house paints, however, and to a lesser extent the use of canvas, not having sacred associations, set painters free to work on a semi-secular basis. Acrylic is easy to use and dries quickly in the hot atmosphere of the desert. Great ingenuity is used in the application of paint. In addition to the sticks used for dotting, there are all sorts of chewed 'brushes' and bits of rag in use.

In 1981, the Adult Education Centre was set up at Balgo to include arts and crafts courses, and students began to paint with synthetic polymer pigments on canvas boards. Writing of Balgo art at the time of the big *Images of Power* exhibition in 1993, Judith Ryan wrote, 'The Balgo artists have developed a distinctive style with a variegated design field and elaborated glyphs that reflect the patterning of body painting, ceremonial paraphernalia and ground paintings. Designs that signify a 'big name' country made sacred by a particular ancestor, or a network of interconnected sites, fuse with the patterns of the background. The symbols are not permitted to stand alone. Often the whole surface is striated with parallel lines which emphasize the dominant glyphs.' There is a tendency, which reflects both Kukatja and Pintupi backgrounds, 'to join dots together into parallel currents of linear designs. Kukatja art is, however, less formal than that of the Pintupi, partly because Kukatja women are encouraged to paint . . .'[6]

The issue of women's right to paint became an important one in the desert communities, partly because of a white conviction that women played only a small part in Aboriginal religion and therefore, it was wrongly assumed, had no right to religious designs (religion and art were still thought, correctly, to be inseparable). 'During the 1960s and 1970s, when Aboriginal art was beginning to be noticed by white Australians, access to art materials was usually denied to women . . . Missionaries and art advisers, it seems, doubted or disregarded the women's religious knowledge or right to paint the ancestral designs of their clan or group.'[7] Craft was the only form of art expected of them.

The women who broke this expectation were Warlbiri women, egged on by a number of white women who took an interest in their work. It happened in 1983 at Yuendumu 'when paintings made for sale began to be produced by the senior Warlbiri women; about thirty of them began to decorate small canvas boards and artefacts with ochre colours . . . In about a year the women managed to save enough

141

money to purchase their own Toyota, enabling access to sacred sites for their *yawalyu* (women's rituals) and other ceremonies.'[8] Their paintings reflected the painting in ochres done upon the shoulders and breasts of women and children during the *yawalyu* rituals.

Women's painting also established itself by another route, as their mythological maps of sacred sites began to be used as evidence in Land Rights' claims. In 1988, a fine exhibition of about sixty paintings by Warlbiri women living at Lajamanu was put on at the National Gallery of Victoria. They had been painted for use in the local school in order to teach another generation about the Dreamings the subsections were heir to. The Lajamanu women became the inspiration for other women artists throughout Aboriginal Australia.

In 1987 the Balgo artists, both men and women, formed their own cooperative – Waylayirti Artists (*waylayirti* is another name for *luurnpa*, the ancestral Kingfisher) – and hired a white coordinator to run it.

Waylayirti Artists believes in a general encouragement of those who wish to paint rather than in selection of the most promising. Robin Beesey, its coordinator, writing in the catalogue for the exhibition *Images of Power – Aboriginal Art of the Kimberley* describes the way art materials are distributed and the ground is laid for the fine work done by the Balgo artists.

> Before stretching and priming the canvases, I go out into the desert communities to visit and distribute them. Upon arrival, I am besieged by artists, their families and dozens of dogs. The most important part then takes place: 'Cheque Book Dreaming'. This is the payment for works sold, or advances on works completed by artists. Advances are called 'tucker money' and are generally $50 – enough for a day's supplies. Then it is time to distribute new canvases and collect finished works.
>
> The artist selects the size of canvas he or she wants, along with a bag of paints, brush and sticks for dotting.
>
> The new canvas is then leant up against the nearest bush or post and the camp dogs visit it in procession to 'mark' it as their own. After this formal camp greeting, the canvas con-

tinues on its way to further abuses. Large canvases make ideal windbreaks, ground sheets, food preparation areas and targets for all manner of substances.

When finally completed, the canvas is put on the roof of the shelter or some other reasonably safe place awaiting my return.

Handover comes when I return the next week and the painting is leant up against the vehicle to enable it to be photographed and the story told. A careful and watchful eye must be kept as the local dogs find it, once again, irresistible and file past to say 'goodbye'.

No doubt trying to encourage local artists to keep at it, and struggling to collect and sell their pictures, makes for a certain cynicism but Waylayirti Artists centre was always full of wonderful paintings collected from the various outstations, and I spent several happy afternoons studying them.

In 1993 a huge exhibition of Kimberley art – *Images of Power* – was shown at the National Gallery of Victoria with a section devoted to Balgo art. There was some annoyance in the Balgo community that the catalogue showed a photograph of a 'humpy' against a desolate desert background as, presumably, representative of living conditions in the remote Wirramanu community. Virtually all the Aborigines at Balgo lived in, or in the hottest weather outside, Government houses, and it was difficult to see the photograph as other than a deliberate misrepresentation.

I very much wanted to buy a painting to take home and eventually chose one by Bridget Mardi Mudjidell, a fifty-eight-year-old painter, which now hangs on my bedroom wall in London. It shows a large lake in the centre, and a creek with three camps around it. There is a bushfire in brilliant red and orange, and also a rainbow which winds snake-like across the top of the painting. On each side of the creek there are bush foods growing, beautifully painted in white and green and red dots, and it is these which tremble in a misty and mystical light and make the painting an endless source of interest to look at, or watch.

Aboriginal paintings must be sold with a 'story', a document which gives information about the painting and the artist, together with a photograph of the painting itself. The story issued with my painting says that Mardi is of the Napanangka subsection and a Jaru speaker. Her painting is of a place called Wanjaltjarra, near Yagga Yagga. 'As a small girl and prior to contact with Europeans Mardi spent much of her time in this part of the desert' reads the paper. 'She has an intimate knowledge of its features as well as the location of precious food and water supplies. This painting shows people out hunting and camping.'

When I showed Brian the painting he went off to find Mardi to introduce her to me. When she arrived I told her how I loved her picture and would take it back to England. Brian asked her if she could say anything about it and she said, with a comprehensive wave of her hand, 'Mother country . . . Granny country,' somehow evoking, as the painting itself does, the deep emotions of the desert world before the white people came. She also went on to mention by name the people sitting round the campfires. (I thought she was giving individual names, but Brian later said that they were subsection or 'skin' names.) With a complete change of mood she then asked me what I had paid for it.

'Quite right!' Brian encouraged her. 'You should know that.' I could see her comparing the price I had paid with the money she would get, and finding the difference unpalatable.

Later I saw people painting on several occasions, usually sitting on the ground and surrounded by others. It became obvious that many paintings were group activities, with members of the family or passing friends obligingly filling in a few dots.

'The acrylic medium,' says the catalogue of the Images of Power exhibition, 'offers artists a complete range of brilliant, permanent colours. The flat, shiny visual effects of synthetic polymer create a sense of brightness or brilliance, a quality admired by Kukatja and Warlbiri artists. Shininess or brilliance is considered to be a sign of health, well-being and beauty and is believed to have emanated from ancestral beings when they first emerged . . . The conjunction of black and white, resulting in harsh tonal contrasts, is used to heighten graphic symbols, enabling the country to be identified from the structural core of the design and the mythological content to be read.'[9] The colour and the contrast, in the opinion of critics, gave the Balgo canvases a 'bold opulence' in contrast to the 'matt quiescence' of pictures in ochre and bush gum done elsewhere.

Later, when I was back in Perth, I returned to the National Gallery to look at the Aboriginal paintings again, and asked to be shown round by one of their official guides. Daphne Wood entered warmly into my enthusiasm, helped me interpret particular features of the paintings, and talked about the particular problems of the 'secret-sacred'. Once, she said, she had been teaching a mixed class of white and black children and had shown them an Aboriginal painting, commenting that, unexpectedly, an aeroplane seemed to have found its way into the landscape.

'That's not an aeroplane!' an Aboriginal child said at once very definitely, and she began to explain how it was a rock formation that looked very like an aeroplane, where it was and what its importance was.

'The next day,' Daphne said, 'she was back first thing saying to me that she was mistaken. Of course, it was an aeroplane! I knew, and I think she knew that I knew, that she had mentioned the matter to her parents, and they had made it clear that she had given away some information that was secret. Of course I accepted what she said without argument.'

I asked Daphne about the work of women painters and she said that she had noticed that they seemed less interested in 'journeys' – in Aboriginal terms usually the heroic journeys of the ancestors – than in static situations, the depiction of the 'camp' and the life that went on there. By chance, there was an exhibition of paintings by white Australian women painters – of the Heidelberg School of Art at the turn of the century – being shown in the same gallery. Going round it later the same day I found myself comparing their subjects – the house, the garden, a child at the piano, the family at dinner, a vase of flowers – with paintings of male painters of the same period, frequently depicting the 'heroic' founding of Australia – by soldiers, graziers, prospectors, statesmen. Their art too, seemed 'more static'. But white women, like Aboriginal women, had been encouraged to concentrate their energies on the home and the family. Would either change?

CHAPTER THIRTEEN

There are only a few ways for *kartiya* to be admitted to the Aboriginal world, and I longed to be able to attempt the most important, that of speaking Kukatja. Only in that way, it seemed to me, was it possible to show a more than superficial interest, to indicate a commitment to comprehension. It couldn't be, of course. I am a timid linguist at the best of times, easily reduced to the sort of 'shame' Aborigines understand so well. That apart, I could see from looking at other *kartiya* around me that in addition to the willingness (which not all of them had), it took patient years and, probably, the kind of situation (which did not obtain) in which I could not get things I wanted – food mainly – without mastering Kukatja pronunciation. The habit of English was too strong not just for me but for white/black relations at Balgo.

I compensated myself by listening to others speaking it wherever I could – it had a pleasant sound. I also enjoyed studying the Kukatja/English dictionary compiled for use in Luurnpa School. The school was bilingual, with Kukatja as well as English-speaking teachers. Some of the adolescent students spoke good English, but the children often lapsed into Kriol, or pidgin. *The Teacher's Handbook* notes some Kriol phrases in regular use: 'It paining me', 'I'll torch you!', 'mine one', 'I'm bin finis', 'I'll off it', so that new teachers might understand what the children were saying.

Like all the desert languages Kukatja was, until living memory, purely an oral language. Then Fr. Anthony Peile began to write it down and, when he died, his work was put into dictionary format by the National Lexicography Project. A linguist, Hilary Valiquette, employed by Luurnpa School, also edited other work of Peile's which was added to the dictionary and the first Kukatja/English dictionary was published in 1993. As Kukatja became a written language for the first time, children in school could learn to read their own stories in their own language.

Kukatja, along with Walmajarri and Jaru, is part of the Pama-Nyungan language family, a group of dialects mutually intelligible because of a large shared vocabulary. Many desert-dwellers speak one of these Western desert dialects, and most can converse in two or three of them. People often refer to their own dialect as a language for reasons of political identity. Kriol is also widely understood between Aborigines who do not have languages in common, but its debased English does not do justice to Aboriginal dignity when it is used in front of white people.

Without understanding the linguistic history, I found myself fascinated by the content of the new Kukatja dictionary. It carries a warning that, having been compiled by Peile as a result of many conversations with the 'old people', all of whom had grown up in traditional Aboriginal life, it does not entirely meet the language needs of the younger generation. But it is its traditional bias which makes it so interesting, an archive compiled just in time, of a world already vanishing.

Just as you would expect, Kukatja is a language full of words mentioning and describing the natural world. There are not merely, as you would expect, a wealth of animals – bat, whistling duck, scorpion, euro, emu, possum, bandicoot, perenty, honey ant, budgerigar, snake, louse, marsupial mouse, mountain devil – but there are fine distinctions, such as *putjil*, 'brown frog with stripe on back found in soft sand', or two different words for a galah (a type of bird), *piyarrku* (the bird by day), or *piyarr-piyarr* (the bird by night).

The vocabulary is the vocabulary of a hunting people, with words for ways of walking silently, or leaving no track (you walk on the heel and outer sole of the foot). There are many descriptions of different sorts of spear wound – *wiiturruly* is 'a wound caused by a spear going right through the arm, leg or trunk, and breaking the skin on the other side'. The dictionary names the particular exhaustion of the leg muscles that comes from prolonged hunting, of the pain in leg muscles that comes from fighting. There is a special word for a straight flight of a boomerang as opposed to the curved flight that returns it to the thrower. There is even a left-handed boomerang for those who need it.

The many words and phrases that describe physical suffering in the dictionary are eloquent of the pain of life without modern aids to comfort. There are many references to stomach pain, leg pain, sun burn, parasites and skin lesions. There are words for 'shaking oneself to get rid of parasites', for 'blindness caused by the sun', for diarrhoea and vomiting.

There are a number of expressions for feverish sweating, for 'the cold sick', and for belching and burping. One who becomes ill as a result of being bitten by a snake – literally 'eye become black' – will 'lie down and become sick, the ground seems to spin round and round. The victim will become sick and stiff, he will get a headache after being bitten.'

Pregnancy has many words to describe its various stages. *Tjurnikurlu* describes the belly of a pregnant woman. The dictionary example demonstrating how the word is used translates, 'A pregnant woman will always go into the shade and remain there.' A newly pregnant woman suffers from *tungun-tungun* – morning sickness.

A baby in the womb that was *tjalpu-tjalpu ngarri* – lying the wrong way – caused concern. *Mirrkatjurra* is to 'give birth to'. *Kuliyakanyila* means both to wait and 'to have a difficult birth'. *Mulkiri* is to have breasts engorged with milk; and *mulkirriwa* is to have milk freely flowing. A newborn baby is *tiintiin*, which also means 'pinkish'.

The dictionary reveals a meticulous knowledge of plants, both the ones that are good to eat and the many that have some healing power. 'Bush tomato', *pintalypa*, is given to people suffering from exhaustion after walking a long distance. It is also good for headache and for difficulty in urinating. Water-lily seeds may be used as a rub to avoid being bitten by leeches when swimming. *Parntingunma-ngunma*, apple bush, is a decongestant – the smoke relieves respiratory complaints, and leaves and stems used as a pillow help those with colds. It also keeps flies away from meat. Box is used to cure boils; grevillia leaf ash is rubbed on sores; Fitzroy wattle, *kampuka*, is a fumigant, and makes an antiseptic paste if moistened with saliva; the desert poplar makes good emergency tobacco, as well as curing a number of ills.

Burns are soothed by being rubbed with a particular kind of bird excrement. The leaves of many desert plants, if macerated and mixed with water, help heal sores. The native doctor may attempt *tiinmarra*, a healing ritual. He will 'place the open hand on muscles and tap with the other hand closed, flick the muscles with index or third finger on the right hand'.

The resourcefulness, ingenuity and commonsense of the desert emerges in entry after entry. The many ways of keeping cool in the murderous hot season, the use of grass stems to clean between the teeth, the use of bark as splint or bandage, as 'bush shoes' and as painting brush, the use of certain roots bound round the feet to protect against hot sand or blisters, the use of a hollow branch to intensify the sound of the human voice in a love song. The desert was playground, house, courting ground, concert hall and hospital.

There are entries, usually giving examples of the way a word or phrase may be used in a sentence, that give sudden vignettes of Aboriginal traditional life. For instance, *tjarntarr-tjarntarrariwa*, to kneel, notes: 'Children will kneel upright or sit back on their knees when expecting their father coming back from hunting.' *Tjarnala* meant 'to carry a larger child or a sick adult on one's back'. Evil spirits – *tjarnpa* – were liable to make you sick, but children were comforted at night by being told that the willy-wagtail distracted the spirits by chatting to them. Children were reared – *tjarlula* – as a result of good songs sung by their fathers. A 'crackling in the nose' was a signal that someone was approaching. (The witches in *Macbeth* had the same idea when they felt pricking in their thumbs.)

The vocabulary observed in close detail the growth of the young, partly in order to know when the boys were ready for initiation. *Tjangarnti* was 'the deep voice of the adolescent boy'. *Tartarrpa* was the word for the breasts of an adolescent girl, and *tartarrnyina* the verb describing their growth. *Tatun* was the word for the small penis of a boy, but it was also a term of abuse for an adult male.

Kukatja is a language that deals with basic human emotions, some of them feelings that the city dwellers, wrongly it seems, assume are peculiar to their unnatural lifestyle. Feelings of loneliness, social awkwardness, jealousy and anger, 'emptiness' at a child going away, all emerge. There are ominous words about being raped. There is humour, sometimes at the expense of the *kartiya* and their 'large red noses'.

Swear words, or words of cheerful insult, as in other languages, very often have an excretal or sexual dimension, as in *Kuna mulurukurukun!* – 'You big heap of shit! Go away', – or the use of the word *pilvi* (the vulva) used much as it is in English.

The strongest feeling left by the dictionary is of the endless struggle and pain of the desert; there seemed to be reference to some kind of pain or sickness on nearly every page. 'The glory' that Geoffrey Bardon had found missing at Papunya was there, in the references to hunting and dancing and love-making and ceremonial activities – these people knew the range of human feelings, both happy and sad – but it was hard, hard, hard. Their life was one of extremes: of heat that burned them and cold that made them tremble, of painful maladies, of severe hunger and thirst and seasons of plenty, of intense activity and blissful idleness. It was a world in which nothing was trivial. They always lived near to death – from sickness, starvation, age, attacks from enemies or from hunted animals.

Reading *War and Peace* under my fan one hot morning, I found myself comparing an experience of Pierre's with that of traditional Aborigines. Pierre, a rich young socialite who has idled his life away with a dissolute crowd of friends, gets caught up in the war against Napoleon and is taken prisoner at the Battle of Borodino. After some searing experiences, including a mock-execution during which he supposes he is about to die, he becomes a prisoner in transition, herded from pillar to post in poverty and need. Unexpectedly, he is transformed from his previous world-weariness and despair.

> While imprisoned in the shed Pierre had learned, not through his intellect but through his whole being, through life itself, that man is created for happiness, that happiness lies in himself, in the satisfaction of simple human needs; and that all unhappiness is due, not to deprivation but to superfluity. But now, during these last three weeks of the march, he had learned still another new and comforting truth – that there is nothing in the world to be dreaded. He had

learned that just as there is no condition in which man can be happy and absolutely free, so there is no condition in which he need be unhappy and not free. He had learned that there is a limit to suffering and a limit to freedom, and that these limits are not far away; that the person on a bed of roses with one crumpled petal suffered as keenly as he suffered now, sleeping on the bare damp earth with one side of him freezing as the other got warm; that in the old days when he put on his tight dancing shoes he had been just as uncomfortable as he was now, walking on bare feet that were covered in sores. He discovered that when he married his wife – of his own free will as it had seemed to him – he had been no more free than now when they locked him up for the night in a stable. Horseflesh was palatable and nourishing, the saltpetre flavour of the gunpowder they used instead of salt was positively pleasant – it was always warm on the march in the daytime, and at night there were the campfires – and the lice that devoured his body helped him to keep it agreeably warm. The one thing that gave him a bad time of it at the beginning was – his feet. Examining his sores by the campfire on the second day, Pierre thought he could not possibly go another step; but when everybody got up he hobbled along, and presently, when he had warmed to it, he walked without feeling the pain, though at night his feet were a still more shocking sight than before. But he did not look at them and thought of other things.

Now for the first time Pierre realized the full strength of the vitality in man, and the saving power innate in him of being able to transfer his attention, like the safety valve in a boiler that lets off the surplus steam as soon as the pressure exceeds a certain point.[1]

Pierre also discovers how wonderful it is to eat when you are really hungry, to drink when you are really thirsty, to get warm when you have been cold, to sleep when tired, or to enjoy a conversation at the right moment. Happiness, he notes, is really very simple. It is about the relishing of the satisfaction of one's simple human needs and not worrying unduly about the constant possibility of death. When *that* happens it will be time enough to yield to it.

It seemed to me that this was the example I was being given at Balgo, what the whole Aboriginal tradition had inculcated. It was not money and the acquisition of possessions it taught, but the more important business of living, of being simply human. And eventually dying.

I remembered a painting by Old Mick Tjakamara at the National Gallery of Victoria. Its title was 'Old Man's Dreaming on Death or Destiny' and its simple, very bold execution showed two windbreaks, with an old man lying by the fire. 'When the old men became frail,' says the description, 'and were unable to keep up with the rest of the group, they would be left behind with food, shelter and water. They very rarely used the food and water but would lie down, practise a form of self-hypnosis, and die. They welcomed their destiny, their return to the ancestors of their totem, from which they had originally sprung to life at their particular conception site or Dreaming.'[2] On the left of the painting is a huge black *tjuringa* which represents the living spirit of Tjakamara; on the left is a red ochre *tjuringa* which is the eternal symbol of the totemic ancestor.

CHAPTER FOURTEEN

One day Anita drove me to Mularn, the outstation on the edge of Lake Gregory. Lake Gregory had burst its banks in the Wet, and a grove of trees stood out in the lake, the waters coming up to their lower branches. The shining expanse of yellow water reflecting the trees and the blue sky was a glorious sight. As always, a number of the Aboriginal women and girls piled into the truck for the ride, and to meet friends and relatives. When the clinic was finished we drove down to the lake, and the girls splashed in the water and began to climb the trees. There were nests in the trees full of budgerigar chicks, and they took the chicks out and began to play with them.

It was ridiculous for me to try to talk to Aborigines about the ways of the desert, but I could not help saying that I feared the mother budgerigar might reject her chicks if they did this. The girls looked at me without comprehension, and I realized they cared very little whether the chicks lived or died. They did not return the chicks to their nests, indeed they probably no longer quite knew in which nest they had found them. Back at Balgo, talking to Anita, I brought up this incident. Was it simply my townie sentimentality to want the little budgerigars to survive? Did the girls see them simply as playthings, and think that if these were lost or broken there would be plenty more where they came from?

Anita felt that the unfeelingness had to do with the damaged and uprooted lives of a people driven out of the desert by a number of pressures. The replacing of the delicate fabric of Aboriginal life in the 'outstation movement', which involved traditional Aboriginal communities reinhabiting the lost paradise of the desert, did not heal the harm that had been done. I was not sure. It seemed to me that white people struggling with racism – myself included – had a need to idealize black people. Then, if they fell short of the ideal, there was disappointment and anger. But to idealize people, just as much as despising or demonizing them, gives them no space to be the ordinary people they are, with their good and bad traits. The final step in closing racial gaps is simply to recognize others as like ourselves.

Someone who was in no danger of idealizing Aborigines was Margie, a woman who came to Balgo to sort out some welfare problems and had no choice but to stay overnight. Hearing my accent she asked what I was doing at Balgo, and then hurried to tell me what she thought about it all. She spoke in the bitter, resentful tones that I had encountered in the cities of Australia but not at Balgo.

'It would have been much better if we had not tried to do anything for these people,' she said when we were alone together, presuming that as a Brit I would agree. 'The Aborigines are a hopeless cause, and attempts to help them is like pouring water into a leaking bucket. They were much better as they were.' (Not all the welfare workers thought like this, I am glad to say.)

I said that the trouble was that 'we' – the Europeans, but mainly the British – had not left them as they were, but had totally disrupted their way of life. Surely that involved some responsibility for what happened? Margie waved all that away as if it were infinitely displeasing.

I was glad she did not stay long enough to hear some of the stories that were swirling round Balgo just then. Like all closed communities it was always rife with rumours, and sometimes they were partly true. There was the rumour, soon confirmed, that 'someone' had broken into the clinic. No drugs had been taken and the assumption was that boys had thought some cans of petrol might be hidden there which they wanted for petrol-sniffing. One of the Aboriginal men had recognized one of the culprits by identifying a bare footprint in the sand outside. All the whites were amazed at the thought of recognizing a fellow-being by a footprint. The Kimberley Health Authority had closed the clinic down as a kind of sanction.

Then there was the rumour that 'our' football team, having gone to Hall's Creek by aeroplane to play a match, had such a merry evening beforehand that 1) they could not play well, 2) did not turn up in time, or 3) did not turn up at all for the match.

Rumour number three was that X's wife had been hugely relieved when he was sent to prison for a long stretch because he beat her and behaved like a tyrant. Her health and happiness had radically improved but now, unexpectedly, he had been released on a legal technicality.

Rumour number four was that a number of the men had hijacked the Kingfisher aircraft in order to get to a football match at Hall's Creek. This was not true. What had happened was that, seeing the little aeroplane take off from the airstrip, and wanting to travel on it to get to a football match, they had stood in its way as it was taxiing down the runway, and forced it to a stop. The pilot, who had a full load, and who had intended to return for the other passengers, said that now he would not return.

Rumour number five was that Madonna, the Aboriginal woman who managed the airline, was so angry at the obstruction of the airstrip that she was closing the Balgo route for the time being. Since this was the only reasonably fast way to get in touch with the outside world – though it only went as far as Hall's Creek – there was consternation.

All these stories were thoroughly chewed over, together with all their possible implications. There were always similar stories in circulation. They seemed much more interesting than most of the news of the outside world that filtered through on Brian's television, though occasional items – the huge IRA bombing in the City of London, for instance – cut through my unnatural calm.

One day, the entire white community held a 'barby' at the Look-out, a wonderful spot at the head of the canyon with a view for miles over the desert; the young teachers were returning from holidays, one had just arrived at Balgo for the first time, and it seemed the time for a general welcome. The smell of the steaks and chops cooking was wonderful, but the second they were lifted from the grill hundreds of flies descended upon them and the most vigorous waving seemed to make little difference. The struggle to keep a bit of untainted food to myself killed the pleasure for me. At Balgo 'barbies' weren't worth it.

What was worth it was the glory of the sun going down over that huge expanse of sand, reflecting on the mesa as it turned it from pink to deepest red. Very occasionally an aeroplane, very high in the sky, could be seen like a moving star. The sky turned from pink to a deep green, and the stars began to appear. There was a feeling of deep calm and silence, the unbroken peace of the desert.

Another more private pleasure, also peaceful in its way, was swimming in the Brothers' backyard. They had an old-fashioned swimming tank – twelve strokes in each direction. It stood beneath an outhouse roof, which meant that the sun never reached it and it was always cold – too cold by Australian standards, but the sort of temperature outdoor swimmers in Britain are used to. In the late afternoon, after a long siesta, it was very pleasant.

As a farewell feast for me, Brian, Robin and I cooked a huge piece of beef we had hacked out of the freezer, and invited some of the Sisters to roast beef, Yorkshire pudding, and as many of the trimmings as we could put together from the tired food in the store.

Real sophistication at Balgo, however, one that was indulged in by the Sisters when they had time off, was to go into Hall's Creek and spend a night or two in the hotel there. I decided to give myself this treat as I made my way out of the desert en route for the old pearling town of Broome away on the west coast.

It cost $100 to get to Hall's Creek by aeroplane (a small single-engined plane in which I felt rather sick, partly because it gave such a close view of the desert, its bare symmetrically ridged floor, the patches of spinifex, acacia and ghost gums, the winding creeks fringed by vegetation). But first I saw the extraordinary sight of Balgo growing smaller and smaller beneath me. The oval of houses, church, school, with the big expanse of sand in the centre, then the view of the canyon and sand surrounding it, then Balgo shrinking until it was no more than a toy encampment in the vast space of the red desert. My eyes filled with tears. Its characters, struggles, rumours, gossip, with the life that teems so abundantly in a small human community, suddenly, brutally, changed perspective and became part of a much bigger world that I understood even less.

As the Kingfisher plane came down on the Hall's Creek airstrip, Madonna – a young, very pretty woman – came out to meet us in her truck to take us into town. One of the Aborigines on board asked her if she would lend him some money to buy a drink. She shook her head. 'I'd go to the moon for you fellas if you asked me, but I won't give you money for drink. It's against my principles.'

Later, I went along to the Kingfisher office to pay Madonna, and she took me aback with an interest in the London theatre.

'What happened to that theatre on the South Bank? What's it called?'

'The National.'

'Did it really have to close down through lack of money?'

Peter Hall's campaign had made its impact at Hall's Creek.

Hall's Creek was a small, simple town. It had achieved brief fame in the gold rush of 1885–6, and then had fallen back into obscurity. But it had a nice little one-storey hotel, with simple, comfortable rooms and a very pretty garden.

At the hotel I swam in the pool and changed into slightly smarter clothes than I had been used to at Balgo. Luckier than the passenger Madonna had reproved, I ordered a gin – the first for weeks – and sat out and drank it in the warm, scented evening. It was delicious.

The next day I went swimming at Rockhole, remembering to rub a stone under my armpits and throw it into the water to warn the snake, so that it would not be tempted to drown me.

A metalled road, incredible sight, stretched away from Hall's Creek towards Fitzroy Crossing and, eventually, to Broome. On the second night, a Saturday, I waited at a local garage for a Greyhound bus to pick me up at midnight for an overnight journey to Broome. Driving out of the hotel in a taxi, I had witnessed a group of drunken Aborigines fighting with the police.

'There's been humbug tonight,' said my driver. 'Well, there usually is on a Saturday.' He made a disparaging remark about an Aboriginal woman whom he said was at the bottom of the trouble. I felt he expected me to despise Aborigines, and was trying to enter my supposed mood.

He bought me a Coke at the garage and hung around for a bit, seeming uneasy at leaving me by the garage. I was glad when he went, though by then his uneasiness had spread to me. There were beaten-up 'rust buckets' driving in packed with people, and drunken men stumbling out of them to buy food at the garage shop.

A young white guy wearing cowboy boots and a stetson came over and stood beside me. With the ease with which conversations start in Australia, he told me that he was on his way to Fitzroy to work on a 'cattle drive', that he was in love with an English girl whose father did not think he was good enough, and that he was a passionate fan of Manchester United. I was glad of his company. A long silence fell between us and I felt that he was turning some idea over in his mind and then he said, 'Don't get the wrong idea about Aborigines from what you see here tonight! They are the best, gentlest people in the world. I work with them all the time and I know what I am talking about.'

Broome is a delectable town with an eighty-mile sandy beach that rarely sees a shark, and a warm, clean, turquoise sea. I could not remember such wonderful swimming anywhere else I had ever been. The town had a humid atmosphere that made the heat much harder to endure than in the desert and I could scarcely bear to get out of the water.

It had the pleasant ease of a successful holiday resort, with good restaurants, wonderful ice-creams and 'smoothies' (a kind of milk shake), and tourist shops selling the local pearls. It was also the home of a very exciting and lively Aboriginal publishing house, Magabala Books. In the old days it had been the centre for many Aboriginal tribesmen, particularly the Bard people, and then later for a flourishing pearling industry, ruled by one or two dynastic families.

In the Broome Museum, there were dozens of souvenirs of pearling society dances, picnics and fancy dress evenings got up by the white folk. But there was, literally, an underside to the pearl industry – the many Japanese and Aboriginal divers who lived on boats on the water and spent their days scouring the sea bottom for oysters. Few of these figured in the Broome Museum, perhaps because their tale was such a terrible one. Stories of exhausted men and pregnant women trying to hang on to the sides of the boat to recover from intervals of diving, and of having their hands beaten by bars to make them go back down, and others of the terrible effect of 'the bends' (the painful and dangerous result of sudden decompression for which methods of prevention were already well understood) drove the missionary Fr. Gibney to install his own boat and employ Aborigines directly.

There was a wonderful bookshop in Broome with a white proprietor who, when she found I had been at Balgo, let loose her scorn on the Catholic Church.

'If you ask me they're half the trouble!' All the same she asked affectionately after Brian. She was an ex-Catholic. Her shop was full of wonderful books about Aboriginal life, and as I went to pay for the ones I had chosen she introduced me to the writer, Pat Lowe, who had dropped in for a chat. Plainly, the interesting people gathered here, and I tore myself away with difficulty.

Many Aborigines were to be seen on the streets of Broome – a number of them having lived at Balgo. In the hot evenings, I saw what I had already seen at Hall's Creek, the gathering of young Aborigines, or drunken older ones, working themselves up to a confrontation with the police. The anger was palpable.

CHAPTER FIFTEEN

I am old enough to remember taking a Union Jack to school on Empire Day and celebrating the way Britain had brought civilization and Christianity to India and Africa, the New World, Australia and New Zealand. Endemic to that colonial way of life, so endemic that it took me years to notice it, was a belief that all the peoples whose countries we annexed, ruled, or invaded were intellectually and spiritually our inferiors, not, as people used to say, 'white men.' Some of them were known to have had high civilizations in the past, some of them were simply 'savages' and were particularly lucky to receive our influence – it was always faintly alarming to see King George or Queen Elizabeth II confronted by their dancing and spear-shaking. What was hidden beneath this benevolent but patronising attitude, was a belief that 'natives', most, if not all of whom had skins darker than ours, were not as human as we were, not quite real, perhaps not human at all. This did not mean that we should be nasty to them, unless we absolutely had to – on the contrary we should bring them justice, kindness, and the delights of our religion – but it was with the strict understanding that what we had was better than what they had, the corollary of which was that we were better than they were. In brief, we were bred to be racist, and the breeding worked all the better since most of us never met anyone with a black or brown skin, though we read adventures in the nursery in which white men got the better of natives, and about greedy Little Black Sambo. I can still remember my shock on first seeing a Negro – a G.I. – when I was about ten, and the surprise, as late as 1963, of seeing people of so many different races walking about in the streets of New York. Of course, I felt benevolent to people who looked different from me – life had given me no reason to be otherwise – but I was deeply, uneasily aware of the 'otherness' and I did not know how to dislodge that feeling. Nothing, not Christian high-mindedness, not liberal beliefs, not political correctness (especially not political correctness) really made the shift for me that made non-white people fully human. What did, slowly, and what must be the only possible way, was first, living alongside many Caribbean people in North Kensington and second, slowly beginning to make friends with people from a different racial background. Gradually, the miasma of difference dissolved like a choking fog.

The sense of difference hit me again, powerfully, when I first got to Balgo. The bridges which humans learn to make with one another – shared interests and experience, conversation, both trivial and serious, obvious similarities – seemed scarcely to exist. Yet, paradoxically, ever since the visit to Kowanyama, I had felt the extraordinary power of Aboriginal life, and the glimpse there of something I needed – both attraction and love. It wasn't that I could truly share it – I could be little more than a timid observer – but I felt there were clues there, poor over-literate Westerner that I was, that I needed to follow.

What happens, of course, with familiarity, is that the strange feels less strange, and one of the oddest, least-expected thoughts I began to harbour was that the people of Wirrumanu were just like every human community I had ever known. This was as surprising to me as if I had time-travelled, say two thousand years back in Britain and, after the first shock at the different way people lived, had suddenly seen that the similarities to the present inhabitants were extraordinary. And this, it seemed to me, was the antidote to the racism in which I, like so many Britons, was brought up. Everything I had been taught about people of other countries (not only black people, either – Wogs began at Calais in those days) had emphasized difference from our British selves. Everything I was experiencing showed exactly the opposite, that human beings are remarkably alike. It suddenly struck me how racists always pick out difference, pretending that people not of their race are less than human, animal-like. This is not only a racial habit either. I remember how once, when I worked in Kentucky, everyone had a conviction that the residents of the neighbouring Indiana were irresponsible drivers and generally hopeless in every way. Residents of New York have exactly the same belief about the inhabitants of New Jersey, and people in Yorkshire and Lancashire like to air very much the same sort of prejudice. Reason and commonsense seem to fly out of the window – identity is secured by despising others. What cannot, must not, be allowed is how very alike people are, even when the external differences are striking. Perish the thought that a suburban family in Wimbledon and, say, a Masai family, have a huge amount in common, but like all humanity they worry about love and fidelity (or the absence of it), about how to bring up their children, about how to wrest a living in a difficult world, about sickness and frailty and old age.

It was not just the generalizations – the big issues – that struck home the sense of familiarity at Balgo. The particular pressures of unemployment and poverty (and poverty was very real there) revealed exactly the same unsuccessful shifts for survival that you could find in any poor housing estate in Britain. There was alcoholism, gambling, domestic violence, occasional robbery of the white folk, fights between men, sickness (much of it the sickness of those who cannot afford to eat properly). Houses were surrounded by a pitiful debris of twentieth-century Australia – bits of cars, bedsteads, plastic bags, cans, bottles, paper. In the old days, the debris a small hunting-gathering group left in its wake would have consisted of wood, bones, ashes, stones, a windbreak made of branches, grass, hair – nothing that sun and wind and rain could not deal with. But consumer durables are indeed durable, almost impossible to get rid of without elaborate methods of collection.

Material conditions apart, though, the Aborigines of Balgo were perhaps luckier than the British poor. They had both a past and even a present that was shot through with a sense of dignity and nobility, with myths and a relationship to the natural world around them. The Dreaming imposed upon them a constant re-enactment and re-experiencing of their myths, and their understanding of the totem made it possible to live not only in their constricted individual human identities, but in the multiple identities of the natural world. Of course, the Aboriginal world many of the older people at Balgo had known in childhood had been fractured irredeemably. Nothing could argue away the fact that, with and without blame, the coming of the white folk had effected a kind of rape upon their primordial world. And yet still the fragments of what the Aborigines possessed – the ceremonies, the ecstatic paintings, the sense of meaning and of sacredness, the astonishing immersion in the landscape – made them enviable and underlined the poverty of Western sensibility.

Back in Perth, waiting to be picked up at the airport, I bought a newspaper, suddenly hungry for the trappings of white culture. The columnist of *The Age*, Les Carlyon, under the title *Lost Tribes of Australia*, began his piece, 'Enlightened folk now say Aborigines would have been better off if they had never encountered whites . . . Not being a social engineer, I don't know whether these claims are sound.' He went on to describe a tribal group, thought to be the last, which wandered out of the desert in the mid-1980s: 'With barely suppressed derision we noted that the seventy-nine-strong clan worshipped a rock.'

Carlyon used this idea for a witty article, noting the number of white men on the Stock Exchange who worshipped rocks, and the Melbourne fans who, every Saturday, painted or dressed themselves in blue and white in order to worship 'a joker who fools around with a scrap of hide inflated with air'.

In the same issue, the Australian Chief Justice, Sir Anthony Mason, defended the Mabo ruling (that Aborigines had rights to traditional lands from which they had been unjustly driven by white pastoralists and miners). This was in reply to a bitter attack from the Western Mining chief, Hugh Morgan, who had claimed that it was absurd to feel guilty about white settlement because 'Aborigines were the weaker culture and would not have survived anyhow.'

In a tabloid paper there was an account of an Aboriginal man being attacked:

> The 60-year-old South Lake man, Clarrie Ugle, claims he was punched and kicked off a Transperth bus by a passenger in East Perth on Monday after the driver refused to accept his all-day bus ticket as valid. Mr Ugle said the driver and an inspector ignored the assault, closed the bus doors and carried on up Brisbane Street before stopping to drop off his

attacker. Mr Ugle, who was bruised and shaken, said the man then ran back and punched and kicked him into a wall and a car in front of several witnesses who did nothing. The attacker, described as Caucasian, and in his mid-20s, ran off and Mr Ugle was helped by staff at a nearby hairdressers who called the police.

'My arm was all wrapped up and covered in bandages and I showed my ticket to the bus driver and he wouldn't give it back,' Mr Ugle said. 'He asked if I had a broken arm and then said he'd break the other one for me. We [Aborigines] get it all the time and I don't think it's right – I don't drink or smoke, I didn't swear or anything like that – I'm a human.' Police confirmed they were investigating the incident and had contacted Transperth to find out the bus number and the driver involved.

Within an hour of being back in mainstream Australia I could feel the mixture of concern and fear, goodness and hatred, guilt and cynicism, with which 'the Aboriginal problem' was treated in Australia. The deep-seated guilt and fear had struck me just before I left Balgo when a visiting Sister sent me a paper she had written about her inner struggles with racism.

We'd rather not know there was a time which we can just touch with our fingertips, and our parents certainly lived through, when there were white people who left the family dinner table to 'go hunting'. All around the table knew what that meant even though they were cobwebbed in silence – Aborigines were to be rounded up and shot, the land cleared of them. More recently, lots of country people can remember the black stockmen and their families camped down by the river and the way they disappeared once legislation (1967) was passed giving them equal pay, for why bother with them and their sloppy ways when you could get white men?

I had read about the 'hunting' of Aborigines, and not all of it in the distant past. In 1926 at Forrest River, near Wyndham, more than a hundred Aborigines were slaughtered as an act of intimidation probably instigated by a fanatical police officer. 'They shootin' that lot now,' an escaped Aborigine informed a missionary, 'picanniny, old old woman, blackfella, old old man'. In Europe, just a few years later, others who were thought to be less than human were slaughtered with the same savagery – babies, old women, men and old men.

In Perth I got to know a middle-aged white woman, Fay, who, as a result of her Christian convictions, felt concerned about what were known as 'fringe-dwellers', groups of Aborigines who live in shacks or caravans on the outskirts of cities and towns in Australia. One such group, under the leadership of an Aboriginal activist I will call Jim, had had their homes burned on a site on the edge of Perth and as a result had nowhere to go.

Fay's (Anglican) church challenged the authorities by allowing the group to camp on the land on which the church stood. The church only had the sort of lavatory and washing facilities that it needed for church socials, and the authorities contested their action by saying that they were breaching health regulations. The Rector stood firm (wanting to draw attention to the homelessness of the Aborigines) and eventually even the Archbishop of Perth got drawn into the argument, electrifying the media by announcing that he would be prepared to go to jail if necessary, rather than turn the group off Church land when they had nowhere to go. A caravan site was provided for the group and, one day, Fay took me along with her on her weekly visit to them, clutching a bag of cakes as a present.

One of Fay's uses to the fringe-dwellers was to make telephone calls on the group's behalf to 'authorities' who paid small attention to Aboriginal complaints, but who listened when a white woman called. Jim's wife, Rosie, held court in her mobile home. Rosie was a matriarch, a woman of monumental build, holding a large family of children and grandchildren together, through the vicissitudes of poverty, fear, police brutality and official neglect. We sat round the table clutching mugs of tea, grandchildren tumbling on the floor, daughters and daughters-in-law chipping into the conversation. In the corner, unregarded by anyone, was a big television screen showing a soap opera full of sumptuous homes in Los Angeles, and stick-thin women perfectly dressed and coiffed.

'Tell Monica about the police!' Fay urged Rosie.

I knew enough by now to avoid catching Rosie's eye, but nevertheless she went into a spasm of shyness, hiding her face in her hands. Distressed at making her feel 'shame' I found myself gently stroking her broad shoulder saying I knew just how she felt, which I did.

Gradually, she got going on her story, which was one of repeated intimidation by the police. The caravanners would be getting on with their lives when a police car would drive up, and several police would get out holding guns which terrified the smaller children. Everyone would be forced out of their caravans – in one case to Rosie's anger and distress, a group of teenage girls who were taking showers at the time and were naked – while the police 'searched' their meagre possessions, looking for weapons or drugs, or whatever excuse suited their action. The men who were present were made to lie on the ground where they were searched and sometimes hit and kicked. Then, quite calmly, Rosie said one of those things that take your breath away but seem everyday to the speaker. 'Donny, my son-in-law, he got kicked in the kidneys by the police. Now he has to go down to the hospital every week and be on a kidney machine.'

Then Rosie went on to describe her simple and infinitely brave method of dealing with such outrages.

'Every time they do something like that, every time they step out of line, I go down to the police station and complain. They know me in there now!'

Even white people, Rosie told me, could get into trouble with the police if they showed Aboriginal sympathies.

'The Rector, he was walking along one day not wearing his collar, but wearing the Aboriginal colours, when a police car pulled alongside him and called him over, "We don't like people like you," they said, "who take the side of the boongs."

'"I'm sorry to hear it," the Rector replied, "but I am a priest and I forgive you," and he made the sign of the cross over them.' Rosie chuckled with pleasure.

Rosie also described to me the moment of vocation when her husband had decided it was time to become an Aboriginal activist leader.

'He was drinking a lot and couldn't stop, and one day he was out in the bush, and way up on the other side of the creek he saw someone – Jesus maybe – who told him he must become a leader for Aborigines. And from that day he stopped drinking and started working for the cause.'

Rosie's mother-in-law had been politically involved too and, when she died, she had been given a huge funeral with a coffin draped in the Aboriginal flag and hundreds of mourners. 'And the police they couldn't do nothing about it!'

Leaving the site in Fay's car I felt the familiar pang I had come to feel around Aborigines and, suddenly, to my surprise, realized I was envious of Rosie. Sitting centred in the middle of her family, fighting her daily battle against white prejudice, owning very little of this world's goods, her life seemed real, complete, not squandered in the exhausting ambition and greed of the West. I feared the sentiment in this, in particular the false reasoning of the 'haves', who wish to believe the 'have-nots' are happy in order to avoid their own guilt. There was nothing to be envied in the style of Rosie's life which had the wretched helplessness of poverty; she deserved to be delivered from it as maybe her daughters or her grandchildren will be delivered. No, it was more that I recognized my own poverty as against her riches – the frantic activism of the West against the gentle stillness of this big, dignified immovable woman. I wondered if, on her routine visits of complaint to the police station, feelings of 'shame' ever passed from her to the red-neck sergeants.

Apart from the extraordinary quality of centredness, of 'having nothing yet having all things', Rosie and her husband revealed, like a section of a tree reveals its whole history, the huge change that had overtaken Aboriginal attitudes to the white people. Friendly white folk were fine, and their support was always appreciated, but a clock had struck some time back and the word was out that the time had come to fight their own battles. Enough was enough. Liberation was in the air, and beyond everything else, beyond even land rights, that meant having the strength, the determination, the self-esteem, to take the future into one's own hands, and to meet the cost of that. It might be unrecognized as yet by people like the bus driver and the local police but their failure to catch the mood of the times would ultimately defeat them.

I am glad that I was given a chance to see a little of a marvellous people, some of whom remembered the old Aboriginal life of hunting and gathering, and the way every moment of life was filled with the wonder and sacredness of the Dreamtime. Like other indigenous peoples they have enormous problems to solve now in trying to find a way to live alongside the producers and consumers of what we like to call the First World, whom even if they wish to do so, they cannot ignore. I cannot think how they will do that. I think that they know things – about the spirit, about humanness, about wildness – that our ancestors once knew to their great enrichment, and that we have forgotten, to our great impoverishment.

In my own life they made, and make, a difference. At the most basic level they forced me to consolidate what was, in many ways, already present in my upbringing, despite its failures – a pleasure in finding the distinctive flavour of humanity in people apparently unlike me. It gave me a deep sense of joy in being human. But the visit did something for me very like a mission in reverse. By the quality of their lives the Aborigines showed me something of the failure of my own life. I knew, what I had only suspected before, a poverty in myself. I lacked their physicality and, like all whom Christianity has touched, which means everyone in our Western world, I had suffered a disjuncture from nature which I believe needs a kind of healing I can still only dimly imagine. In the great European culture that worshipped the printed word I had been trained to scorn the primordial image and the power of the myth. And, most humiliating of all, I could not sit still, not unless I was 'occupied'. I could not simply commune with myself by myself for hours, and so could never know the special tranquillity out of which the deepest kind of understanding is born. To know the lack is, in part, to guess at the wealth the West denies itself. For me, the task is only just begun and will take me the rest of my life. And if my Christian forebears are to be believed, beyond that.

NOTES

CHAPTER ONE
1. *The Songlines*, Bruce Chatwin (Jonathan Cape, London, 1987, p. 15)
2. *The Rainbow Serpent*, Robert L. Gardner (Inner City Books, Toronto, 1990)

CHAPTER TWO
1. *The Doors of Perception*, Aldous Huxley (Harper & Row, New York, 1954, pp. 12–17)
2. *The Songlines*, pp. 16, 17
3. *Desert People – A Study of the Warlbiri Aborigines of Central Australia*, M. J. Meggitt (Angus & Robertson, Sydney, 1962, pp. x, 27)
4. *The Journal of Colonel Peter Egerton Warburton* (Royal Geographical Society, London, 1874)
5. *A Secret Country*, John Pilger (Vintage, London, 1992)

CHAPTER FOUR
1. *The Fatal Shore*, Robert Hughes (Collins Harvill, London, 1987, pp. 8, 9, 54)
2. Ibid.
3. *The Rock and the Sand*, Mary Durack (Constable, London, 1969, p. 21)
4. *Remembering Babylon*, David Malouf (Chatto & Windus, London, 1993)
5. *Mysteries of the Dreamtime*, James Cowan (Prism Press, London, 1989, p. 5)
6. Durack, op. cit.
7. *The Journal of Colonel Peter Egerton Warburton*
8. Ibid.
9. Ibid.
10. Ibid.
11. Ibid.
12. Ibid.
13. Ibid.
14. Ibid.

CHAPTER FIVE
1. *Jilji: Life in the Great Sandy Desert*, Pat Lowe with Jimmy Pike
   (Magabala Books, Broome, W. Australia, 1990, p. 112)

CHAPTER SIX
1. Lowe, op. cit.

CHAPTER SEVEN
1. *The Dreamtime Book: Australian Aboriginal Myths*, C. M. Mountford
   and Ainslie Roberts (Rigby, 1973. p. 9)
2. 'The Land is Sacred', unpublished thesis by Sister Adele Howard,
   RSM, pp. 35, 36
3. Ibid.
4. *Tjarany Roughtail*, Gracie Greene, Joe Tramacchi, Lucille Gill
   (Magabala Books, Broome, W. Australia, 1992, pp. 2, 34)

CHAPTER EIGHT
1. Lowe, op. cit., p. 112

CHAPTER NINE
1. *The World of the First Australians*, Ronald and Catherine Berndt
   (Aborigines Studies Press, 1992. p. 166)
2. Meggitt, op. cit., pp. 282–309, 312–316
3. *Women's Rites and Studies*, ed. Peggy Brock (Allen & Unwin,
   London, 1989)
4.

CHAPTER TEN
1. Lowe, op.cit., pp. 47, 48
2. Ibid.
3. *Aboriginal Men of High Degree*, A. P. Elkin (Australasian Publishing
   Co. Pty. Ltd., 1944, p. 48)
4. Ibid.

CHAPTER ELEVEN
1. Durack, op. cit., pp. 282, 291
2. 'Assimilation Problems, the Aboriginal Viewpoint', T. G. H.
   Strehlow, University of Adelaide, 1961

CHAPTER TWELVE
1. 'The Art of Balgo' by Judith Ryan in *Images of Power – Aboriginal Art*

    of the Kimberley (National Gallery of Victoria, Victoria 1993, pp. 86–93)

2. ' "The gift that time gave" – Papunya early and late' by Geoffrey Bardon, in *Mythscapes – Aboriginal Art of the Desert*, ed. Judith Ryan, funded by Victorian Health Promotion Fund.

3. Ibid.

4. Ibid.

5. Ibid.

6. Ryan, op. cit.

7. Ibid.

8. *Paint Up Big – Warlbiri Women's Art of Lajamanu*, Judith Ryan (National Gallery of Victoria, Victoria, 1988, p. 9)

9. Ryan, *Images of Power*

CHAPTER THIRTEEN

1. *War and Peace*, Leo Tolstoy

2. *Images of Religion in Australian Art*, ed. Rosemary Crumlin (Bay Books, NSW, 1993. Description by Judith Ryan, p. 180)

INDEX

Index